T0162135

BORN FOR WAR

BORN FOR WAR

ONE SAS TROOPER'S EXTRAORDINARY
ACCOUNT OF THE FALKLANDS WAR

TONY HOARE QGM, MID
WITH GERAINT JONES

WELBECK

Published by Welbeck
An imprint of Welbeck Non-Fiction Limited,
part of Welbeck Publishing Group.
Based in London and Sydney
www.welbeckpublishing.com

First published by Welbeck in 2022

A CIP catalogue record for this book is available from the British Library

ISBN
Hardback – 9781802791389
Trade Paperback – 9781802791396
eBook – 9781802791402

Typeset by seagulls.net
Printed and bound in the UK.

10 9 8 7 6 5 4 3 2 1

At length did cross an Albatross,
Through the fog it came;
As if it had been a Christian soul,
We hailed it in God's name.

[...]

The many men, so beautiful!
And they all dead did lie:
And a thousand thousand slimy things
Lived on; and so did I.

I looked upon the rotting sea,
And drew my eyes away;
I looked upon the rotting deck,
And there the dead men lay.

[...]

I closed my lids, I kept them close,
And the balls like pulses beat;
For the sky and the sea, and the sea and the sky
Lay like a load on my weary eye,
And the dead were at my feet.

From *The Rime of the Ancient Mariner*,
Samuel Taylor Coleridge, 1798

CONTENTS

Author's Note   ix

1.   Called to Arms   1
2.   Over the Water   25
3.   Who Dares Wins   43
4.   Badged   59
5.   Assassins   69
6.   The Calm   95
7.   The Storm   117
8.   The Raid   133
9.   Pilgrims   167
10. Retake the Islands   181
11. Troop Attack   225
12. The Final Day   241
13. The Butcher's Bill   249
14. Homecoming   259
15. After War   271
16. A Final Word   287

Acknowledgements   305

AUTHOR'S NOTE

I was born for war.

I can tell you this with certainty and with no shadow of doubt. I've never wanted anything else. I've never been better at anything else.

Every person has a calling. Some spend their lives searching for it. Others know it from childhood, but their life's purpose seems always out of reach.

I was lucky. From when I was a little boy I knew that I was on this earth to carry a rifle. I wanted to do it for my country. Later, I would do it for money. In my time I have been an infantry soldier, a special forces operator and a hired gun. I served in three wars with the SAS, each campaign different to the last, but all with one thing in common: we needed to kill the enemy before they killed us.

This book is primarily about my time in the Falklands War – the aim of which was to reclaim British territories from Argentinian occupation. It is a story of raids and battles, and victories and loss. It is a story about elation, disappointment, anger and pain. I've been involved with many acts of war. Witness to many more. As a member of D Squadron,

22 SAS, I had a privileged position in the task force dispatched by Great Britain to retake the islands in the South Atlantic. I was with the force that retook South Georgia. I was on the raid at Pebble Island. I fought on the Falklands. And, almost like one of the journalists in the task force, I was afforded a good amount of freedom between our special forces missions, roaming the many ships that we operated from. I talked to the crews. I watched the helicopters work. I cheered the Sea Harriers as they took off into the attack and watched them return victorious.

It was a short war, but it was *my* war. It confirmed who I thought I was and what I wanted from life. War showed me people at their best and at their worst. War taught me lessons on what is important and what isn't.

War made me a better person.

I'm grateful for what war gave me, but of course, there is a cost for everything and D Squadron paid a heavy price for our 'adventure'. This book is dedicated to the brave men who didn't come home and the courageous families who must carry that loss. All of us in D Squadron wanted to be there – there was no one who had not volunteered again and again to be in that position – but a soldier's wishes are not always shared by his loved ones. While I do believe that my comrades' deaths were a sacrifice made on behalf of their nation and fellow citizens, I also know that there is no place on earth those men would rather have been – they died doing what they loved. That is something to be grateful for, because few people ever get to find their true calling, let alone get to live it.

Like my comrades, I was born for this life. Not everyone is made to be a warrior and that is a good thing. We need balance in our own lives, in our families and in our society. Our communities need carers and teachers as much as our countries need warriors. There are many different paths in life and I hope that in reading this book, it will encourage you to embrace and chase your own calling, whatever that may be. And I hope that it teaches you something of soldiering and about those who answer the call. I don't pretend that war is glorious, but neither will I pretend that I did not enjoy it. My aim in this book is to be honest and to recall the wars to the best of my ability. I may not be perfect in my recollection, but I say what I say with honesty and with respect for all those involved – I owe that to my brothers.

Some people will ask if it is the place of a special forces soldier to write his account. To them, I would say this: I joined the regiment because I had heard what SAS founder Colonel Sir David Stirling, OBE, DSO and his men had done in the Second World War. As much time has elapsed between my writing this and the Falklands, as had elapsed between the Falklands and the Second World War. I'm not giving anything away that can be used to harm British forces. Like every special forces soldier I've signed the Official Secrets Act and more, but there are no secrets in this book, only untold stories. In one way or another, all of the information in this book is already out there. I am simply telling it from my perspective. Hopefully, lessons can be learned and heroes can be remembered.

In my eyes those heroes are the war dead and there were many of them in the Falklands, including friends and comrades of mine. Every arm of the British armed forces paid a price. Operation Corporate, as the mission to liberate the islands was known, was a true tri-service operation that required our country's best on land, at sea and in the air.

I will be the first to tell you that special forces operations were not the deciding factor in the war: without the Royal Fleet Auxiliary and Royal Navy, we would never have got there; without air power, our losses would have been catastrophic; and without infantry, we would never have driven the enemy from their trenches. I hope that my admiration for the efforts of all the services comes through in this book, because I hold all in the highest regard: it was a true team effort and one we can be proud of.

After the narrow but decisive victory at Waterloo in 1815, Wellington remarked that the battle 'was a close-run thing.' So was the Falklands War and in its own right, retaking the islands was as much a pivotal moment in British history as Wellington's triumph over Napoleon. It was the last campaign where Britain acted alone and with the patriotic support of the nation behind her. We haven't seen the like again and perhaps we never will, but that's a conversation for historians and scholars. This book is the boots-on-the-ground story of a soldier and his comrades, based on diaries that I kept at the time and written as much to help put my memories and thoughts in order as anything else. I thank you for reading it.

Swift and Bold,
Tony Hoare, 2021

1

CALLED TO ARMS

If you had met my father after the Second World War, you would never have guessed what he'd done against the Nazis. He was a placid man. A quiet one, who never raised his voice. He was reserved, you might say. He wasn't one to offer advice, but I always knew that he loved me. He was always there, singing cowboy songs or encouraging me to look at the stars.

I didn't know it at the time, but looking back, I expect that he learned how to recognise the constellations when he joined Bomber Command in 1938. The war hadn't started, but everyone knew that it was brewing. Hitler was taking bites out of Europe and it wouldn't be too long before he turned the Wehrmacht's teeth on Poland, bringing Britain into the war, and my dad with it.

He was a flight engineer and I don't know much about his service. He didn't really speak about it. Most of them didn't, did they? I expect they wanted to put the whole thing behind them. Hard things need to be done in times of war, but for a gentle soul such as my father, it must have been incredibly hard for him to live with the knowledge that he contributed to the death of German civilians. Not all sacrifices are physical. Sometimes a man has to give up a part of his soul to do what needs to be done.

It was from my mum that I got the most detail and even that just left me with more questions than answers. My dad's bomber was shot down over Belgium, but he managed to bail out and avoid injury. At one point he was hiding in a quarry as the enemy searched for him – presumably the Gestapo (secret police) and German soldiers.

Not all captured aircrew made it to prisoner of war camps. Some were killed out of hand, but fortunately my father escaped and was helped by resistance fighters along the way. He was taken through what were known as 'the rat lines', a series of trails and safehouses through the Pyrenees and to Spain. From there, he was able to ship back to Britain, though he would never be allowed to fly against the enemy again – the risk was too great. The RAF worried that if a man had used the rat lines, and was shot down a second time, then he could be tortured and give up the escape routes. Given that being part of a bomber crew was the most dangerous British role in the war, there was a high chance of this happening. Nonetheless, I'm sure that was hard to stomach for a man with a strong sense of duty.

There was only one time when my dad talked to me about the war: I was in my twenties, and I was driving us up the motorway to Hereford so that he could visit the regiment. It was night and the orange lights of the motorway stretched away into the darkness. My dad was quiet and then he said: 'The lights remind me of Dresden.'

I had no idea that he'd taken part in that massive raid ordered by Arthur 'Bomber' Harris in 1945. Eight hundred aircraft flew over the German city, dropping almost 3,000 tonnes of bombs. Some 30,000 people were killed, most of them civilians.

What was my dad thinking when he saw those motorway lights and thought back to that night over Dresden? How many friends had he lost? What did his crew think about the raids that they were a part of? Did they talk about it? Was it even possible for a young man to comprehend? Would he do it all again?

After Heathrow Airport was built, my dad was offered a job as a flight engineer on the civilian airlines but he turned it down. As far as I know, he never flew again after the war. He pressed plastic in a factory and seemed quite happy. I believe that he loved his country, but he never beat his chest about it. He was part of that generation who just got on with things and never complained – at least not within earshot of me.

Certainly, Dad never tried to stop me from following my own path into the military. From as early as I can remember, there was never any doubt in my mind that I was on this earth to be a warrior. While I do think that it's possible to turn people into soldiers, I believe a certain few of us are born to be warriors. Maybe it's in our genes, maybe it's in our souls. I don't know. All I can say is that I didn't ever have a choice about being a soldier – it was my fate and a fate that I welcomed with open arms.

As a kid, I was always playing soldiers with my mates. I even had myself a little 'camp' at the bottom of the garden. I was happier outside than indoors, not that I was trying to escape anything – I have no complaints about my childhood. None. I was given freedom, but I was made aware with that freedom came responsibility. I was taught right from wrong. I was left to my own devices and I didn't choose to steal or misbehave and smash windows. I chose to play soldiers in the garden and then, when I was old enough, I joined the local Army Cadets, where playing soldiers came with supervision and often chances to visit actual army barracks and use their training areas.

I'll always be grateful to the cadet instructors who gave up their time so that I could meet more like-minded people and get an insight into shooting, map reading and other parts of army life. In fact, it was on a cadet exercise that I first met an SAS trooper. My guess is that one of the instructors had asked him to come along to talk to us and help out on one of our little exercises. He was in 21 SAS, one of the Territorial Army branches of the regiment, and when he lit a cigarette and buried the match, I thought it was the coolest thing that I'd ever seen – where can I sign up?!

Today, all kinds of information about the military is just an internet search away. That wasn't the case in the sixties, but I did tune in to the news every night so that I could see what was going on in Northern Ireland. Of course I didn't understand and most of the footage seemed to be of British soldiers being pelted with stones, but it was action and I wanted to be a part of it.

I wasn't much of a reader except for *Commando* magazine. I loved Sergeant Rock and that fictional character probably moulded me as much as anyone else when it came to my earliest thoughts about the military. Of course, I looked up to my grandfather. He'd been a 'Bootneck', as the Royal Marines are known, serving on Royal Navy vessels during the First World War – he was stone deaf because of the noise of the ship's big guns. Uncle George was in the Royal Army service corps and uncles Ray, Mike and Ricky followed in Grandad's footsteps and became Commandos. The Royal Marines have done pretty well out of our family!

My favourite of my dad's brothers was Uncle Ray, who served in 42 Commando and later the Royal Marine Reserve. He'd tell me stories from his service, and about Commando missions in past wars, such as the Cockleshell Heroes and the Heroes of Telemark, both exemplary stories of brave men fighting against all odds. We'd do physical training together to get me ready for my own military life, which to the whole family was a given. Ray was a lovely bloke and I looked up to him because he'd been there and done that. He'd missed out on seeing combat, but anyone who goes through the longest basic training in the world has shown they're made of tough stuff.

I imagine Ray was very disappointed that he never got to face off with an enemy, but that's how it goes with the military. War comes and goes like the tide. Conflicts are inevitable, but not everyone gets their feet wet. Ray was unlucky that he missed war and yes, I mean it when I say 'unlucky'. Some might think that's controversial, but believe me when I tell you that people don't become Commandos in the hope that they will see out their career in peacetime. As I said, a certain number of us are born to soldier. Born for war. That doesn't make it right and it doesn't make it wrong, it just makes it a reality. People can protest against war all they like – that's one of the rights that we fight to protect – and I think it's important that we always have a balance in society of people who think differently. Without doubt, some wars have been fought for the wrong reasons, but that's not for the young soldier to know at the time. We have to put our trust in the country's leaders, and hope that the decisions they are making are the right ones.

When I was a kid, I knew that the life I was choosing would be filled with hardship. If I needed my eyes open to the truth of how hard the world can be, though, I got it in my early teens, on a trip to Germany with the Army Cadets.

We were visiting Sennelager, a British base on the Rhine, but it was an excursion to Bergen-Belsen concentration camp that will stay with me forever. You could feel in the air that something terrible had taken place there. The air felt dead and still, there were no birds, but it was a piece in the museum that particularly turned my stomach – it was a lampshade made from human skin. What kind of evil people could do such a thing?

Going around the camp, I was well aware that this would have been the fate of my own family under the Nazi regime. My mum's side of the family is Romany and some estimates put the number of Romany gypsies killed during the Holocaust at 1.5 million. That someone would do this to innocent human beings made me more determined than ever to be a soldier and fight for what was right.

My mother and father had met at a dance in Wiltshire during the war against the Nazis and were married in 1945. Mum lived for her five kids. She'd lost her beloved mother at an early age and I think this made her appreciate her own children even more. That, and she was just an extremely caring person. She was what's known in her community as a 'fae', meaning she was more in tune with the spiritual and supernatural world. Although she didn't practise anything to do with it, she felt things. She knew that my father had been shot down before the authorities told her, and later, she would see something that would open my eyes to the possibilities of what we don't know.

Like a lot of people who have lived on the edge of life and death, I have a very open mind about such things. I can't tell you exactly what I believe, because I don't know myself. I don't give much thought to it, though, because I feel like some things are bigger than us and beyond our understanding.

When I was about eight years old, we visited family and I slept in a room where a baby had suddenly died (I don't know for sure, but I expect it was cot death). My mum woke to the sound of me choking. She said that when she woke up, she saw the baby's face. I remember waking up out of breath and I was certainly shaken by the experience. You can draw your own conclusions as to what happened. As I say, I keep an open mind.

Despite the fact that, like I said, it seemed an inevitability I'd join the military, my parents never tried to push me down any particular path in life. They passed on a basic moral code, one that most of us are given and some choose to ignore. My parents taught me that we have a duty to stand up for our country and people who can't stand up for themselves. They told me that it's wrong to steal, or go through life begging. By example they taught me to work hard and not complain. I would say it was an old-fashioned British upbringing – get on with it and be grateful, and I was. We lived in a semi-detached council house and didn't have enough money for a car, or holidays, but that never bothered me. So long as I had some-where to play soldiers, I was happy.

Sports was another early passion of mine. I was a good athlete and could run the 100 metres in 12 seconds. Like most English boys I played football during breaks and after school, and I was also into basketball. That was rare in the country at the time, but we had a Polish sports teacher who introduced us to it. There were American forces up the road from us at Ruislip and we joined the league with their teams. Sometimes we'd eat on base and that was my first insight into how well the American military feeds its members, with an endless supply of everything from steaks to milkshakes.

My mum believed in big families and so I had a couple of brothers, but we were never really close. One was ten years older than me and the other ten years younger, and we just didn't spend that much time together. The youngest was a bit of an acting protégé and Mum thought he could be a star, so we upped sticks and moved to Hammersmith so that he could attend an acting school there. Things started well, with a spot on a Milky Bar advert and a role as a Crimean refugee in *Upstairs, Downstairs*, but then he was caught with a copy of *Playboy* at the school and kicked out. That has always seemed a bit harsh to me: what happened to 'boys will be boys'?

I also had two older sisters. Like my older brother they went to grammar school and because I was the first in the family to attend a secondary modern, they looked down their noses at me. I wasn't really bothered as I had no desire to go into an academic career. My heart had always been set on the army, and the infantry in particular, and those recruiters were much more interested in my physical performance than my academic achievements.

As far as I knew, I couldn't join the army until I was 17 years old. This turned out to be (as we say) bad intelligence, as the army had its junior leader programme for 16-year-olds, but I didn't find out about that until I was a recruit at Winchester. Before Winchester, though, I thought I had a year to fill between leaving school with a few O-levels and taking the Queen's shilling, as accepting service in the armed forces is known.

This would turn out to be the longest year of my life.

* * *

I've never been to prison, but the closest I've ever felt to it was working as an office clerk right out of secondary school.

It was at a company involved with transport at Heathrow and I soon realised that I was not made for nine to five or spending all day indoors. I felt like a caged animal. I'd always been happy in life up to this point, but this felt different. Though I was never diagnosed – who talked about mental health back then? – I soon found myself becoming depressed. I was lethargic. I was constantly in a bad or low mood. I knew that I was in the wrong place and doing the wrong thing. That doesn't mean that everyone else there felt the same, of course. Some people seemed very happy in the job and good for them – we're all individuals. If you thrive in an office, great, but for me, it felt like a life sentence:

Get up.

Go to the office.

Watch the clock.

Go home.

Go to bed.

Repeat.

Repeat.

Repeat…

I just couldn't do it.

Even with my 17th birthday providing a light at the end of the tunnel, I still couldn't hack the thought of another six months in the office. I had to get out and after 180 days of mind-numbing monotony, I left the job. A lot of my school mates had gone into similar work and continued in it until they retired. So far as I know, they didn't hate it. Life takes all types.

Around then, my sister Beverley had moved up to Scotland with her partner Alan. For a long time she'd tried the office life herself, but it wasn't for her either. With the money she saved doing the job, she opened a small stables, where people could rent stalls for their horses. My sister had had her own horse for years before that and I'd learned to ride it. Fortunately for me and my mental health, she agreed to give me work with her and so I would groom the horses and muck out the stables. It turned out that I was a lot happier shovelling shit than filing paperwork!

I enjoyed my time in Scotland, but my goal had never deviated from joining the army. One thing I will say about the stables is that horses are temperamental animals and so that gave me great experience when it came to dealing with the army training staff that I'd soon encounter!

And that day was fast approaching. A recruiter had told me that I should join the Royal Green Jackets (RGJ) as they were locally recruited from London. They had a storied history, being descended from the 95th Rifles who had fought under Wellington, including the legendary defeat of Napoleon at Waterloo. I liked the idea that the Green Jackets were a bit different to other infantry regiments, who they referred to as the 'Heavy Mob' or 'Redcoats' because of the colour of their ceremonial uniform – a throwback to the day when Britain's line infantry wore red tunics to disguise the sight of blood.

During this time the Vietnam War was at its peak and more combat footage was on TV every night. Strange as it sounds, I felt like it was a tractor beam pulling me in and so one day I travelled with my mate Malcolm into central London. We arrived at the US Embassy and a US Marine asked us our business:

'We're here to enlist, sir.'

He smiled. 'How old are you?'

'Sixteen, sir.'

'Come back when you're eighteen.'

I don't know if it was even possible for us to enlist in a foreign military, or if that Marine was just trying to get rid of us. Either way, we went home with our tails between our legs. It was only a temporary setback, though – Malcolm would eventually join the Royal Armoured Corps and on my 17th birthday I walked into the local recruiting centre, signed on the dotted line and took the Queen's shilling.

It was finally time to become a soldier!

Before I could be sent to a training depot I had to attend a three-day trial at Sutton Coldfield. There, we were given medical examinations and had our fitness tested by the physical training instructors. The lads I became friendly with at the selection course had all signed up for the Parachute Regiment, who do infantry work and parachuting, and so I asked the staff if I could change my choice of regiment. I was told that it wasn't possible – maybe because they didn't want to do the paperwork? – but even though I'd asked, I wasn't really bothered. So long as I could be an infantryman, I'd be happy.

I got my wish in 1973 and when I arrived at basic training, I can honestly say that I wasn't afraid in the slightest of what was to come. I was just excited. This was my dream. I had nerves, but these came from wanting to be the best that I could be. Later in my career, the army ran a recruitment campaign that was short and simple – 'Army, be the best'. That's exactly how I felt when I walked through the gate at Peninsular Barracks, Winchester, home of the Light Division.

Pride is an important part of any functioning organisation and perhaps nobody does it better than the regiments of the British Army. When you join up, you're not just joining the people who are currently serving, you're continuing a tradition.

You're becoming part of a family. At least that's what they tell you. Like any family, it has its ups and downs!

Peninsula Barracks, a vast complex of stone buildings, had been built during the Peninsular War era (1808–14). Several platoons were in various stages of basic training and I joined the men who would be filtered into the three battalions of the Royal Green Jackets (RGJ). The Light Infantry (LI) were also a part of the Light Division, but they had their own training platoon and battalions. The RGJ and the LI would later be amalgamated to form The Rifles regiment.

The formation of a rifles unit can be traced back to the American War of Independence (1775–83), where British commanders were impressed by the use of unorthodox enemy sharpshooters. War is often a copycat's game and in 1800 the Rifle Regiment was introduced to the Baker rifle, which was unlike the traditional smooth-bore muskets issued to the units of the line at that time. Trained to fire up to four rounds a minute, a great emphasis was placed on marksmanship, meaning: skilled and accurate shooting. New skirmishing tactics were developed and proved to be invaluable in the Peninsular War. The 95th Regiment provided the rearguard to the British Army during its 'Retreat to Corunna', the Dunkirk of its day. The regiment proved invaluable to the Duke of Wellington and fought in some of the pivotal points on the battlefield at Waterloo.

When I joined their ranks, it was 60 years since the Light Division had fought in the slaughter of the trenches and 30 years since they had fought against the Axis powers. To say I was humbled to belong to such a lineage was an understatement. The 'soldiering first' mentality that I'd experience in the Light Division, with an emphasis on fieldcraft and infantry skills rather than spit and polish, would serve me well in my own campaigns. But right now, I didn't know that. All I knew was that I had to get through training first!

* * *

People have an image of basic training being all shouting, screaming and endless punishments and that's probably true of a lot of people, but I never experienced it myself. Our instructors treated us like adults and I think we became better soldiers because of it.

We had three corporals who were in command of a section apiece, which is standard practice in an infantry platoon. We recruits were split down into the three sections. We had an officer who was nominally in charge, but we saw little of him as he was mostly concerned with our administration. Day-to-day running of the platoon came down to our sergeant, who was easy-going and quite a comedian. He was a black Londoner, pretty rare for the army back then. Most of the lads were white and working-class, but the sergeant's race wasn't an issue. A sergeant was a sergeant and we respected our NCOs (non-commissioned officers). Indeed, we aspired to follow in their footsteps.

There were no trashed lockers, or beds thrown out of windows. We were taught the art of soldiering in the same way that you'd teach a boxer. Yes, things were hard. Yes, they were physical. But our training was all conducted with a very common-sense approach, each lesson building on the last, with confirmation that we understood the previous steps before moving on to the next one. I enjoyed this methodology and threw myself into it. Our NCOs fostered a sense of competition between sections and platoons, which is vital when you're trying to build pride, cohesion and a sense of belonging to something bigger than yourself. Men are tribal and nowhere in Britain is that sense of tribe stronger than in the army.

Despite being new we were encouraged to voice opinions, even if what came out of our mouths was 'bone' – meaning 'stupid' or 'dull'. The Light Division wanted thinking soldiers, which makes sense when you consider the history of skirmishing, where soldiers of all ranks have to make decisions on their own and act with initiative.

I found the physical side of training very easy. I'd pushed myself hard before coming to depot (training barracks) and it paid off, and not just directly, in terms of being able to physically complete the challenges. The fitter you are, the easier it is for you to pay attention to what you're being told, as well as being able to operate smoothly and efficiently despite working at a high tempo.

Fit body, fit mind.

I was very keen and eager, which is what they want to see at depot. You're expected to know how to do the job above you in the army and for obvious reasons – if that person gets hit, someone needs to step up and take over. In fact, part of the orders process is to establish who will take over from whom in case of casualties. Some might find that morbid, but again, it's just realistic. People die in war and more people die if you're not prepared to react to that in an instant.

My favourite part of the 14-week course was the live firing package at Brecon. This was where we tossed live grenades and assaulted positions as our fire support put suppressing fire down right in front of us. It was the greatest adrenaline rush I'd experienced in my life so far. If you don't enjoy that kind of work as an infantryman, then you're in the wrong career.

The other soldiers in my platoon were a mixed bunch, from all walks of life. One of the blokes was in his thirties, which is quite funny now that I think back on it – he was almost twice my age! We had a few villains in there – the army was a way for them to get some distance between themselves and trouble – and we had one lad from London who stabbed a local on the same day that we were issued with our clasp knives. He got kicked out of training, which didn't bother us, but we were gutted to learn that we would all be losing our knives as a result. It was my first introduction to an important lesson in the army: when one person makes a mistake, everyone pays for it. The days of being an individual were over.

The 14 weeks of depot flew by and before I knew it, I was standing on the parade square in my number twos – the khaki ceremonial uniform of the army. We wore peaked caps, our boots looked like mirrors and we had rifles in our hands with swords fixed – we don't call them bayonets in the Light Division, thank you very much!

Also, we don't march at the same pace as the heavy mob. Light infantry drill is a lot faster, a throwback to the days when skirmishers would go ahead of the main force. Little details like this really help foster a sense of regimental pride. We loved the fact that we were now British Army soldiers, but we were even more proud to be Green Jackets.

My mum and girlfriend both came down to see me pass off, as graduation is called. I say 'girlfriend' – really, she was just a friend, but she was the best-looking one that I could think of inviting and I wanted to make a good impression.

Apparently, though, I had managed to do that on the course. One of the NCOs told me that I was on the shortlist for Best Recruit and I got a little excited that the prestige might be mine but in the end it was given to the oldest guy in our platoon. I didn't leave empty-handed, though, having won the marksmanship award, which is given to the best shot. I do wonder if they gave me that award because they knew how keen I was and they didn't want me to be overly disappointed at not getting Best Recruit.

But they needn't have worried. I had realised my dream of becoming a soldier and it was without doubt the best day of my young life. So far, the army was everything I'd hoped for.

That changed quickly.

* * *

With some of the other lads from the training platoon I was assigned to 3rd Battalion, the Royal Green Jackets, who were based at Shoeburyness Barracks in Southend, Essex.

As a new bloke, I expected to get a bit of a rough welcome. I was young, but I wasn't naive. Still, I was very disappointed to learn that the battalion would be deploying on a four-month emergency tour of Northern Ireland and I would not be joining them. Policy stated that you had to be 18 to die for your country on Operation Banner and I would still be 17 when they deployed. I hoped that I would be sent out to join the battalion on my birthday, but when I asked, my hopes were dashed. I was told that I'd remain as a member of the rear party, who would be carrying out supply and guard duties back in the UK, and that hurt.

Maybe I wanted to prove a point that I could soldier and soldier well. I threw myself into the training exercises that the battalion was carrying out to prepare for the tour and I did such a good job that the platoon commander pulled me out in front of the platoon, singling me out for praise: 'This is how I want it done! Why is a new bloke doing it better than the rest of you?'

Well, you can imagine how that went down – first, I found my mattress and other items in a filled bathtub. Then, one night when I was taking a piss, someone smacked me across the back of the head with a broomstick. I got in a few scuffles, but I knew that I wasn't Sergeant Rock from the *Commando* magazines – I couldn't take three or four of them on at once.

My antagonists were the older Riflemen who had lost their sense of keenness, if they'd ever had it at all. Some people join the army to soldier, but others join because it's a steady paycheck.

Liam Kelly was one of these blokes, and he enjoyed making my life a misery by messing with my possessions, insulting me, and getting on the physical side of things. He was a Scouser and he seemed to take a dislike to me from day one. The feeling was mutual, and still is. I've got no time for bullies. Never have, and never will.

Fortunately for me, I didn't have to put up with him for long. The battalion shipped off to Ireland and I started my job in the rear party. It was at this time that I met my first trooper from 22 SAS. His name was Bruce and he had been returned to the Green Jackets for a reason he never shared. Of course, I pestered him with questions about life in the special forces. Already I was thinking about where my career might take me.

For now, that was Cyprus. Rear party was dull work and I wasted no time volunteering to try out for the division's shooting team. The trials took place in Dhekelia on the island of Cyprus, and I absolutely loved it. My keen attitude was rewarded and I was selected for the team in the role of gunner on the General Purpose Machine Gun (GPMG), a privileged and envied position, depending on who you asked – not everyone liked carrying the extra weight of the gun and its ammunition. The GPMG is still in service today, which says a lot about what a great design it is. Some things you just can't improve upon and the GPMG has served British soldiers well in war after war.

In 1974, not long after we left Cyprus, the island was invaded by Turkey and it remains split to this day, with a UN force keeping the peace.

Back in the UK that year, our shooting team was selected to represent the army in an international competition held in Aldershot. There were teams from Iran, Pakistan, the US and other places, but we took the trophy. It was a great time and my last chance to catch my breath before life started moving a lot more quickly.

It was in Strensall, North Yorkshire, out drinking with the blokes, that I met the woman who was to become my first wife. A council estate rat like me, she worked in the local Woolies. Things moved quickly from there – I didn't know it then, but we had set out down a hard road.

At that time in my life, things seemed to be looking up. In 1974, 2nd Battalion were gearing up for a tour of Northern Ireland and needed more blokes. To my delight, I was transferred out of the 3rd Battalion and joined 2 RGJ up in Catterick, Yorkshire.

2 RGJ had been a resident battalion in Northern Ireland, which meant a two-year stint rather than the usual four-month emergency tour. They'd lost guys and had been on the barricades during Bloody Sunday. The year 1972 had been arguably the height of the 'Troubles', as the conflict was known, and I was glad to know that I would be going across the water with experienced soldiers. Despite knowing that the battalion could suffer casualties, I was gagging to see action. The way I saw it, it's always the other guy who gets hit, right?

2

OVER THE WATER

The winter of 1974 was fast approaching and with it, my first tour of duty. The 'Troubles' in Northern Ireland began in the late sixties and officially ended with the Good Friday Agreement signed on 10 April 1998 after negotiation between the UK government, the Irish government and Northern Ireland's political parties. Of course, the violence wasn't just confined to the province: terrorist attacks and murders were an ever-present threat on the UK mainland and even beyond. More than 3,500 people were killed during this 30-odd year period. Just over half of this number were civilians, a third were security forces and 16 per cent were paramilitary groups. Republican paramilitaries, notably the Provisional Irish Republican Army (PIRA), were responsible for 60 per cent of the deaths, loyalist paramilitaries 30 per cent and the security forces 10 per cent.[*]

It was a dangerous place and, little known to many people now, the British Army first took to the streets to protect the

---

[*] 'Sutton Index of Deaths: Summary of Organisation responsible'. *Conflict Archive on the Internet (CAIN)*. Ulster University. Archived from the original on 21 July 2015. Retrieved 24 February 2016.

province's Catholic population. The Ulster Volunteer Force (UVF), a loyalist organisation, had carried out a number of petrol bombings on Catholic homes, schools and businesses. Designated a terrorist group by the British government, they remain so to this day.

Of course, there were people who wanted a united Ireland, but others just wanted equality. One of the major grievances was that the Protestant leaders of the province were disproportionately allocating money, leaving some Catholic areas of Belfast as slums. A civil rights movement began in the mid-sixties, with marches in the city. Bombings were carried out on water and electricity installations, leaving civilians without essential amenities. In 1969, British soldiers were deployed to protect such facilities.

At first the soldiers were welcomed by many in the Catholic population and squaddies could be seen drinking tea with the locals in Belfast's toughest estates, but it was only a moment of calm before the storm.

Violence began to spiral out of control in 1969. There were clashes between rioters and the Royal Ulster Constabulary (RUC). Protestors died of their injuries. A young boy died of gunshot wounds sustained from an RUC armoured car. Politicians on all sides made angry addresses to the television cameras. RUC officers were murdered. 'Peace walls' began to be built between the rival parts of Belfast.

Over the next couple of years the violence peaked. Riots, murders and bombings were regular occurrences. Perhaps the most infamous day was Bloody Sunday, 30 January 1972, the echoes of which are still heard today.

Religion is often blamed for war. It struck me that in our battalion we had people of several different faiths, but it wasn't something that was made an issue of. What came first was the brotherhood. We looked at what we had in common, rather than what we did not. Personally, I've never bought into the idea that religion is to blame for wars. I believe that power-hungry people are the real cause of war. They use the excuse of religion as a way to provide a justification for their actions and to manipulate others into carrying out the violence that then benefits the leaders. Like most things in life, things are rarely black and white.

The Troubles were in the news every day back then, so there was no one in our battalion who didn't know what we were going into. Of course, many of the blokes had first-hand experience, having been out there for two years at the height of the conflict.

I was confident in our leaders. Our sergeant major was a good one, fair and skilled in his job. Our platoon commander was Rupert Pritchard, which put a smile on our faces – a 'Rupert' is the nickname for an officer in the British Army because so many of them share that name. Our very own Rupert was a big strapping bloke who looked a lot like my childhood hero, Sergeant Rock. He wasn't one of the lads, but then it wasn't his job to be. If you don't notice an officer then they're probably doing a good job and clearly he was a skilled soldier – after transferring to the Parachute Regiment, he became aide-de-camp (personal assistant) to General Sir Mike Jackson and eventually became the commanding officer of 22 SAS.

Over the water we'd be operating in four-man teams, known as 'bricks', which was basically a section split in two. I'd command one brick, while our full corporal, Tony Smith, would command the other – he'd also command both bricks when we worked together. Tony had been shot by a terrorist gunman on the last tour in the province and so he wasn't quite as enthusiastic about going as I was.

My best mate at the time was 'Taffy' Williams, a Welshman and a real character, who kept me on my toes every day. A great athlete, Taffy had played rugby for Neath before he signed up. We were such good mates that he'd even come home with me when we were on leave. He truly was a brother-in-arms.

Just before we deployed we had a few days to spend with our families. I visited my mum and dad, but thankfully there weren't any theatrics. Though there was danger in Northern Ireland, it didn't feel like going to war. My girlfriend wasn't quite so calm about the whole thing, however. Not because she worried I wouldn't make it back, but because she didn't want to spend four months alone. At the time I thought she was selfish, but looking back, it's understandable. Some people really don't want to be alone and while I had the brotherhood, she was far more lonely back home. While most couples are getting to know each other in their first year together, I was about to be away for four months.

After the short pre-tour leave we travelled by train up to Liverpool docks, where we boarded the Royal Fleet Auxiliary (RFA) merchant vessel *Sir Lancelot*, which would take us across the Irish Sea. While I knew what awaited us would not be the stuff of *Commando* magazine, I was excited all the same. I wanted to be deployed with a rifle in my hand, wherever that may be.

* * *

The first weeks in Northern Ireland felt bizarre, to say the least. The places we patrolled looked like any other rough council estate in Britain, only there were burned-out cars, burned-out buildings, rubbish in the streets and graffiti and pro Republican murals on the walls. It felt like your average British town, but in an alternate universe.

By the time that I arrived the days of the Catholic locals being friendly to British troops were long gone. We were shouted at, spat at and generally treated like shit on a shoe. You could feel the hate and hostility in the air.

Our company was based in McCrory Park in the Whiterock Road area of West Belfast. This part of the city led into Ballymurphy, a hive of paramilitary activity. Both areas were rundown and it's fair to say some parts were slums. It was quite clear that tax money had gone on improving Protestant areas and while I never forgave the violence, I could understand the resentment of the residents. Still, we had a job to do and so we got on with it – searching people, houses and cars at vehicle checkpoints. The threats we faced were mortar attacks, improvised explosive devices (IEDs) and shots from gunmen and snipers.

Having been hit on his last tour, Corporal Tony Smith always looked like a nervous wreck before we 'hard targeted' out of the gate to go on patrol. Hard targeting was a case of running out as quickly as possible and finding cover, because the entrances of patrol bases made great targets for snipers. As the saying goes, 'stay low, move fast'.

I didn't ever think less of Tony Smith because he was spooked. Quite the opposite, in fact. He might have been scared but he never once shirked his duty. That, to my mind, is the definition of courage: being afraid, but doing it anyway.

Taffy didn't ever seem scared to me, but he could be a bit of a loose cannon, as he proved one day when we stopped a man on the streets.

'What's your name?' Taffy asked him.

'Mickey Mouse.'

Well, if that was meant to be a joke Taffy didn't get the punchline and he put his fist into the guy's face.

It wasn't unusual for someone to get roughed up if they tried to play the tough guy and so I didn't think much of the incident until we were called before our commander. Apparently 'Mickey Mouse' was a 'tout'. Out of all the people in West

Belfast, Taffy had punched an informer. They were like gold dust in the area and so when Mr Mouse complained to the RUC, the chain of command came down heavily on our brick and we were all sent to court.

I'm not sure who came up with the plan – probably Taffy – but someone suggested that we should all march into the courtroom wearing knee-length trench coats so that we looked like German storm troopers. Well, you can imagine how that went down, but as it turned out, we were only given a telling-off. I expect it was all just a show to massage Mr Mouse's ego so that he would keep snitching.

During the time I was on my first tour, there were a couple of pieces of news that really caught my attention. The first was that two PIRA bombs had gone off in pubs in Birmingham, killing 21 people and injuring 182. All of us were livid, of course, but we had some Brummies in the battalion and these lads had to be gated so that they didn't go out onto the streets with hot heads. The second piece of news came in a letter from my girlfriend. Well, about to be *ex*-girlfriend. It was what we called a 'Dear John' letter – a letter telling a deployed soldier that he is dumped. She didn't want to be with someone that she didn't see, so that was the end of it.

I can't say I was heartbroken, but my ego was certainly bruised. To try and laugh it off, I pinned the letter to the door of our accommodation so that everyone could read it. The lads took the piss, but laughter is often the best medicine.

The 'Dear John' was the nail in the coffin in what had proved to be a disappointing tour for me. After four months of monotonous patrols and guard duty the battalion was going home. We hadn't lost a man, which of course was great news, but I hadn't had the action I craved. In later years I would come to appreciate this gradual learning curve, but at the time I was frustrated and wanted to get a proper crack at an enemy.

That time would come.

* * *

As a young lad, and a soldier to boot, it's fair to say I had a lot of pride and more than a little ego. And so, when we returned to the UK at the end of the tour, I went to see the girl who'd dumped me and convinced her to give us another try. Deep down, I knew that we were better off without each other, but my ego made me override that common sense – I didn't want to fail at *anything*.

Of course, I now realise that walking away from a bad situation is not failure. In fact, it's one of the biggest wins that you can give yourself *and* the other person. Oh well – just another of those things that has to be learned through experience! At the time I convinced both her and myself that we should be together, which resulted in a tumultuous few years to say the least and would almost cost me my dream.

But all of that was in the future. At the time I was miserable with my partner, but I loved my job and I felt as though things were going well in my military career. I'd only done one tour, but I seemed to soak up soldiering like a sponge. Some people can pick up a guitar and figure out the chords, I could figure out warfare. It came naturally to me. When I looked at terrain, I don't know how, but I knew the best approaches to assault a position – I could just see it. I also benefited from great instruction, something the British Army excels at and why we have done so much with small armies. If you were looking for the 'pound for pound champ' of the infantry world, my money's on the British squaddie every time.

Our little army had given Britain quite an empire at one time and we still held on to parts of it around the world. One such place is Gibraltar, a strategically important base with a port and an airport. Famous for the size of its massive rock – a labyrinth of tunnels and caverns that can be held by very few men – 'Gib' sits at the mouth of the Mediterranean and is still claimed by Spain, who lost it to the Bootnecks (Royal Marines), back in 1704. You'd think 300 years is long enough to get over a defeat, wouldn't you?

Apparently not and to that end a garrison is maintained on Gibraltar at all times in order to prevent the Spanish from occupying the colony. In 1975 it was 2 RGJ's turn to provide the infantry contingent and you might think this sounds like a great deal for a soldier – Mediterranean weather and beaches – but believe you me, after two years on a three-mile-long island, you start to go a little crazy. In 1969 the Spanish had closed the land border and it remained that way for 13 years, including the two years we were there in the mid-seventies, so there was no way of 'stretching your legs' beyond The Rock. It felt as though we had been sentenced to a prison colony, although admittedly, we were prisoners who spent a lot of time in the bars. The locals here were a lot more friendly than they had been in Northern Ireland, and there was no doubt that they were glad of our military presence. They did not want to be occupied by Spain, and that made them forgiving of the often loud and drunk soldiers who were there to make sure that that didn't happen.

As luck would have it, at that time we received a new unit training officer (UTO) from the SAS and the commanding officer instructed him to put all of the lance jacks (lance-corporals) back through an intensive cadre. The gruelling training was conducted in Gibraltar and also in Brecon, mid-Wales, during December and I was determined to win my stripe back. The 'cadre from hell' was by far the hardest thing I'd done in the army up until that point and we were constantly soaked, freezing and exhausted.

At the end of the course, we were sent back to The Rock and those of us who had passed the course were called out on parade to receive our stripes. I couldn't believe it when I didn't get just one back, but two – I'd been made up to full corporal! I was 19 at the time and I reckoned I must have been one of – if not *the* – youngest full screw(s) in the army. I was so proud, I probably grew six inches overnight.

The NCO cadre had shaken a lot of the soldiering cobwebs off me. British Army infantry units rotated bases every two years and another unit came to Gibraltar to take over the monotonous guard duties from us – they could have the pleasure of sunshine and confinement to a rock for the next two years! There remains a garrison on Gibraltar to this day, but relations with Spain aren't as bad as they used to be and the land border is now open.

As 2 RGJ were relocated to Britain, I was feeling fit and motivated, and just as well – our battalion was going back across the water and this time, we would be heading for Bandit Country.

* * *

In the mid-seventies, in Northern Ireland, the insurgency largely moved out of the cities and into the rural areas. I expect this was because the paramilitaries didn't want to alienate the residents by getting them caught in crossfires and so on. South Armagh – known to soldiers as 'Bandit Country' – had become the most notorious area and that's where we were heading.

I couldn't have asked for a better bunch of men to be deploying with. The only fly in the ointment was the officer commanding (OC) our company. If I'd been born for war, he'd been born for painting on canvas. He was a well-connected proper gentleman and while we were on tour, he invited the BBC out to join us. We were tasked with escorting them around Forkhill while they filmed him painting!

All in all, he seemed far more concerned with what was on his canvas than leading his men into the fray. Like most of our officers, he came from a 'good' family, with money and land. This worked in our favour as he took the company to his family's estate and we used the large area to work on our counter-insurgency drills, such as patrolling and vehicle checkpoints. The OC pulled in the locals to help – whether out of patriotism, or because they worked for his family, I don't know – and this did help our training. You had to treat these actors as 'civilians' and not just beat them up, as we did our mates from other companies when they filled the roles!

One day, the OC set up a 'serial' involving a farmhouse in a valley. A serial is basically a mini exercise that's usually used to train and test smaller elements of the company, like sections and fire teams (eight men and four men respectively). You take turns going through the serial, which can obviously take a lot of time when dealing with a company of men. In a nutshell, a serial is a way of confirming that you have understood the prior training given to you – in this instance, how to react to enemy fire in a semi-rural environment like the British countryside.

From the sound of the blanks firing beyond the trees, it became quite obvious what was happening to the teams as they approached the farmhouse: they were being ambushed. There was only one track up to the building, which sat in a steep-sided and narrow valley. It was a perfect killing ground.

Well, when my turn came, I ignored the track and took my men up and down the hill. It was very hard going, but we entered the back of the farmhouse without anyone knowing and took the 'gunmen' prisoner without a shot being fired – it was exactly how you'd want a patrol like that to go.

But not the OC, apparently. He was angry that I hadn't 'played the game' and had gone up the track. The only game I was playing was to win and I didn't see what was to be gained by doing one more 'reaction to enemy fire' drill. It's just a hunch, but I always felt like the OC begrudged me holding the rank of full corporal at such a young age – most of the others in our company were in their twenties. I wonder what the OC's thoughts were of Alexander the Great, who conquered the Persian empire at 18 years old. Whatever the case, we were stuck with each other.

At least for now.

The second tour over the water in 1977 passed largely like the first. We conducted patrols, checkpoints and searches. The biggest difference was that the enemy actively tried to kill us, including a mortar attack on our guard post. I was on patrol with my men at the time, so we could only watch as the scene unfolded. Fortunately, there were no casualties in our company, but when the bomb disposal unit came out to check over the truck that had been used as the bed of the mortars, the technician set off a bomb hidden in the truck's engine and was seriously injured.

Our battalion didn't come away from the tour unscathed, either. One Rifleman spotted a PIRA flag and asked permission from his corporal to retrieve it. Unfortunately, the flag had been placed to lure a soldier into a trap and the resulting explosion cost him his life. I don't think the corporal ever forgave himself for falling for such an old trick. To any soldier reading this book: if you didn't put it down, don't pick it up.

Fortunately, I didn't lose any of my own men, but that wasn't for their lack of trying. Our small guard post was positioned on an estate and one of the council house windows that faced us would be filled every day by 'Sadie', who would put on a show for the troops. Unbeknown to me, one night two of my Riflemen snuck out – unarmed! – to visit her. Thankfully, Sadie was not a honey trap and the lads were not murdered with their pants down. Both were charged and sent to Colchester's Military Corrective Training Centre, however, and I took a lot of heat from the OC. I may not have known what they were up to, but I was their section commander and so I was given a big slice of blame to put on my plate. It was probably for the best that the lads were sent to Colchester because I was ready to beat some sense into them both!

Despite our tour taking place in winter, I enjoyed the patrolling that we did in the rural areas – I felt like we were doing some proper soldiering. There was always a sense of danger to the area. Infamy, even. Our beat included the Three Steps Inn in Drumintee, where British intelligence officer

Captain Robert Nairac was abducted by the IRA on 14 May 1977. The man was known as a bit of a loose cannon who would travel around the area with nothing but a pistol and a bad Irish accent. One night in the pub he got into a fight and was 'lifted'. No sign of him was ever seen again, but he was reportedly 'interrogated' (tortured), killed, put through a meat grinder and fed to livestock. There is a fine line between brave and foolhardy. Whichever he was, his end was not a good one.

As well as losing the Rifleman to a boobytrap, there was more tragedy in store for our battalion. Our close observation platoon (COP) had come under contact and was engaged in a fierce firefight with gunmen. Our CO (commanding officer) – beloved by his men – flew in a Gazelle helicopter to take control of the scene, but the pilot made an error, stalled the aircraft and it ploughed into the ground just south of the border.

Ignoring the fact that British soldiers should not cross into Ireland, the COP platoon moved fast to secure the scene and give first aid to the pilot and our battalion adjutant. Unfortunately, there was nothing they could do for our CO.

The news of his death was a blow. He was the man who had awarded me my corporal stripes and a leader to look up to.

Not so our OC or our battalion second-in-command. When the latter arrived at the company, I was enraged by his apathetic attitude. He wanted us to keep a low profile until we left the province and went home. *We* wanted to get out on the ground, find the people who had engaged the COP and kill or capture them – with a preference on 'kill'.

'Keep a low profile' wasn't what I wanted to hear as an infantry soldier. The infantry's mission is to close with and kill the enemy. If I couldn't do that in the battalion, then I'd find somewhere I could.

Fortunately for me, Britain had just the regiment.

3

WHO DARES WINS

think it's fair to say that at the time of writing, the Special Air Service (SAS) is one of the most famous military units in history. In the Global War on Terror, everyone has come to know about the US Navy SEALs because of the 2011 raid that killed Osama Bin Laden and big Hollywood movies like *Lone Survivor*. The SAS went through a period like that in the late seventies and early eighties. When the regiment struck back against terrorists, the people of Britain, who lived in fear of bombings, understandably saw them as heroes. Then there was the famous Iranian Embassy siege of 1980, which didn't need a movie – the world saw the successful hostage rescue on live TV.

Of course, within military circles, the regiment already had the highest reputation. They only took the best and then they made them even better. America's secretive Delta Force was based on the SAS model. So too was SEAL Team 6 – their premier unit in hostage rescue and their choice for raids on the highest of high-value targets.

Although the British Army was constantly rotating battalions through Northern Ireland at this time, it wasn't the deployment that many of us wanted. Patrolling the streets expecting to be sniped at or bombed made us feel like we were constantly on the back foot. Like many others, I wanted to join a regiment that dictated the terms of the battle.

That ethos of striking at the enemy was exemplified by the founding father of the SAS, David Stirling. His vision was that small squadrons of highly trained soldiers would strike behind enemy lines, taking out key installations and demoralising the Axis enemy. Such actions also aided the effort on the front lines because the enemy must divert men and resources to protect their rear.

The SAS got off to a bumpy start, but by the end of the Second World War they were an indispensable part of Britain's arsenal. Book after book has been written about these exploits. By the time that I was a Rifleman, the SAS had been fighting all over in the remnants of Britain's empire. They fought battles in places like Malaya, Aden and Oman. These were the kind of shooting wars that I wanted to be a part of and so I told my wife about my plans.

She wasn't very receptive to the idea. Indeed, it's fair to say that she didn't want me in the army at all. Due to the high tempo of operations and training in special forces I was guaranteed to be away from home even more.

Taffy thought it was a good idea. He knew how keen I was on soldiering, but he had absolutely no intention of joining me. Comfortable in the battalion, he wasn't going to volunteer for extra work.

As an SAS soldier – and indeed, as a Rifleman – you are expected to act on your own initiative. No one put on a pre-course to teach me the ropes and I didn't ask for one either. Instead, in every bit of spare time that I got, I would take my map, compass and bergan (a military rucksack) to the Brecon Beacons and become familiarised with the area, pushing myself hard up and down the hills. My fitness levels were as high as they'd ever been, but my wife did not appreciate my absences and when I was home, things were sour. That, of course, just made me spend even more time on the hills so that I could be away from the confrontation. The term wasn't in use at the time, but 'toxic relationship' summed us up perfectly – I was miserable at home, I was happy on the hills. It was as simple as that.

I would not be put off my goal of becoming a special forces (SF) soldier and so in the summer of '77 I made the drive to Sterling Lines, Hereford, for the very first time. The camp was on the outskirts of the city and didn't have anything like the grand stone buildings of the Napoleonic-era Peninsular Barracks. This camp dated to the Second World War and was made entirely of wood – they don't build them like they used to!

My first point of contact in the SAS was actually a civilian who would administer us on the course. He was an SAS veteran himself and a grumpy bastard. Through him, I was assigned a barrack room and equipment. We would carry a drill FN rifle for the course – a decommissioned weapon that couldn't fire.

Like most courses in the army, we began with a PT test. It amazed me that some of the men failed this. If you know the standard for a course, why would you turn up if you can't reach it?

Next, we were introduced to milling. There's probably a technical definition, but to put it simply, they pair you off by size, give you boxing gloves and tell you to punch the shit out of each other's heads for a minute. It wasn't a pass-or-fail event, but they were looking for men with natural aggression who wouldn't back down.

They also threw us in a pool, fully clothed and wearing belt kit, to make sure that we were at least somewhat capable of not drowning. I'm not a great swimmer and to be honest, I would rather have been punched in the face for another minute instead of trying to tread water. In the end I had to get inventive to pass the test – I'd let myself go underwater, then push back up off the floor with my toes.

Everything to this point had just been tick-in-the-box exercises to make sure we met the basic criteria. On day three, we got our first real challenge: the Fan Dance. The Fan Dance was a timed march with 40lb kit that took place in the Brecon Beacons and involved ascending Pen y Fan, the highest mountain in South Wales – twice! Instructors led the way and set the pace, so all I had to do was stick with him. It was no walk in the park but my training paid off and I didn't have any difficulty keeping up. A large number of men fell out at this point and again, I was surprised, especially by those in the infantry – what had they been doing in their own regiments? Why weren't they prepared?

The next two weeks were focused on instruction. We did PT but we weren't beasted (pushed very hard), so that we would be coming into test week fresh. I thought the instruction was a good idea as it gave everyone a decent chance of passing the map reading so long as they could keep their heads and work without supervision.

Test week was what people really think about when it comes to selection. It demands skilled map reading and physical tenacity as you are required to hit certain checkpoints at certain times. To do so, you must average a pace of 3.5–4km an hour, which might sound alright, but remember, this will be up and down mountainous terrain, sometimes at night, and you have a full load on your back and a drill FN rifle in your hands (slings aren't allowed).

All that being said, I had no fear of failure, being young, fit, well trained and confident. I finished the first test – an arduous timed navigation over the mountains in full kit – without complications. A solo route march around the mountains doesn't make for great reading, though, so let's move on and just say I was one step closer to becoming a special forces soldier – I knew that I would pass.

That all changed with a phone call.

* * *

I was called into the office of the course administrator. Getting pulled into anyone's office is rarely a good sign in the army, but I couldn't think of anything that I'd done to get returned to my unit. I'd been working hard, finishing towards the front and rarely opened my mouth unless asked to.

What was this about?

'You need to call your family immediately,' the administrator told me.

All kinds of thoughts were running through my head as I dialled the number. It was my mother-in-law who answered: 'You need to come home at once, Tony. She's had a nervous breakdown.'

It was like I'd been punched in the stomach. I was so close to passing this first stage of selection, but what choice did I have?

'Sir,' I told the administrator, 'I need to drop out.'

After handing in my kit, I drove like a madman to my home. This wasn't just because I was worried about my wife, but because I was so angry and frustrated to have to leave the course. Maybe if this had happened in the first two training weeks then I could have been given a day or two to go home and come back, but on test week? No chance. As soon as I handed my kit in to the stores, I was done. Still, I knew that I didn't have a choice, I had to get back to my wife. I could only imagine what kind of state she'd be in after a breakdown. Things didn't seem quite as bad as I'd imagined, though, and at the time I felt that I'd been dragged away from selection and prevented from completing the course.

I took my things and left. I realised then that I should have let things end years ago, but my ego had stopped me. Now I was paying the price: my pride had robbed me of my dream.

The worst part about it all was that I had to return to my battalion a failure. No one asked about the circumstances of why I dropped out. They probably assumed I couldn't hack it and I didn't correct them.

I could have given up then. I could have said, 'Maybe it's not meant to be,' but I didn't, for I was as determined to join the SAS as ever. After a few months cooling my heels doing the usual guard duties, lessons and exercises that are the day-to-day of life in an infantry battalion, I was on the next selection course.

This time, there was no stopping me.

I'd spent a few miserable years with my wife where we both brought out the worst in each other and we were separated when I went back to Hereford the next summer. It was like I'd cut away an anchor and I completed selection's test phase on the second go without any issues. The only dampener was that my fellow Green Jacket had not passed the hills with me. He'd actually finished the final test within time, but because more men had passed than expected, they'd raised the bar. I still don't understand this mentality, to be honest: if we had enough men who could meet the special forces standard, why not bring them in? It's not like we can ever have enough good operators – sabre squadrons are constantly undermanned.

I'm glad to say my fellow Green Jacket still went on to have a great career, rising to lieutenant colonel, which is incredibly rare for a man from the ranks.

Arriving back in camp in the back of a four-tonne truck, those of us who had passed selection week were met by the training wing's OC –- a man who would later be targeted at home in a PIRA attack. Fortunately for the regiment, the terrorists failed in their attempt.

After the selection phase, there were about 50 of us left for what was known as continuation training, which is really just the basics of soldiering – weapon handling, marksmanship, fieldcraft and tactics, for example – done to a high degree. Some of those who had passed had come from corps outside of the infantry and so a lot of the time was spent bringing them up to a high standard in those bread-and-butter soldiering skills. I was in my element and enjoying every day of it.

As part of the selection process we were sent to the jungle, which I was particularly excited about. They didn't have one of those in Hereford or Brecon and so most of the trainees would be going to Belize, while a few of us would travel to Brunei. The reason for this split was because there was a cap on the number of soldiers who could be in Belize at once, given there were still hostilities going on there.

I loved the jungle from day one. It's the ultimate training ground for an infantryman as you have to be right on top of your drills and your personal administration. We did everything from learning survival techniques to counter-insurgency (how to beat insurgents), micro navigation (how to map read to a high degree), long-range patrolling (how to move tactically over long distances) and reconnaissance (how to gather information, often from under the noses of the enemy). This was the Sergeant Rock adventure I'd been looking for!

I was very lucky to go to Brunei as it was with D Squadron, SAS, as part of their pre-deployment training. Looking back, I wonder if the 12 of us who were sent there had been chosen because we were in the top percentage of the trainees, as the lads in Belize were constantly beasted until their numbers were reduced to fit a quota. All 12 of us in Brunei would get badged, while many of those who went to Belize would not.

It was at this time that I met Louis, the local tracker who helped teach the art to the SAS. A lovely bloke, he would later be awarded a well-deserved MBE for his services. He was also something of a craftsman and like the other men, I bought a machete from him – I still have that 'Parang' to this day.

The jungle training included patrolling, navigation, contact drills and more. We lived out of our bergans (rucksacks) for long periods and worked on our close-target recce skills. Reconnaissance is the key to successful actions and a large part of the SAS workload. If you don't know where your enemy is, in what strength and what he's doing, any attack is doomed to failure. Whether the SAS are putting in the attack themselves, or passing the information on to other units, good 'recce' is key to military success. Special forces movies are all about blowing off doors and abseiling down buildings, but a lot of SF operations involve lying in the dirt for days on end, slowly building up a picture of what the enemy is doing. It doesn't make for a great film, but it does make for success on the battlefield.

Of course, information gathered is useless unless you can send it back to your commanders and so once we had gathered the intelligence it would be sent back via a Morse code-trained radio operator. That didn't mean we could escape signals training, however, as we all needed to be able to communicate and send reports over the radio using open and coded transmissions.

One moment I will never forget is when our tracker set a trap at night and in the morning, we discovered it had caught one of the jungle's elusive wildcats. There was no sign of the creature itself, however – just its leg. It had chewed it off to escape. To those of us who wanted to soldier behind enemy lines, this was a sobering reminder of the brutality of nature and the law of the jungle.

Our final exercise in Brunei was a live fire attack against an 'enemy' camp. We patrolled through the jungle and then waited in our final positions until dawn. During this time, I provided a delicious banquet to the jungle creatures – every insect and his dog came out to have a bite.

When things got noisy on the attack, meaning the bullets started flying, I enjoyed every second. We assaulted the camp, taking out the 'enemy' positions with grenades. Everything that I had joined the army to enjoy! I hoped this was just a taste of what was to come.

Just because we hadn't been RTU'd (Returned To Unit) by the end of our time in the jungle didn't mean we'd be badged into the SAS and so once we left the trees and returned to Hereford there was a tense time waiting to learn if we would be allowed to continue on to the final phase. Some people were let go because their soldiering skills weren't of a high enough level, others because of character issues.

I made the cut, which meant there was only one more hurdle in front of me.

Escape and evasion.

*   *   *

The All Arms Combat Survival course is known in wider circles as 'escape and evasion'. Obviously, working behind enemy lines there is always the chance that we might become compromised and if that happened then we needed to know how to evade capture. We also needed to know what it would be like to *be* captured and what might happen when they tried to break us. Notice how I didn't say that we were taught how not to break, because that's not something that can be taught to a person: you either will or you won't. This course would just weed out the ones who would break more quickly than others.

As grim as that part of the course would be, the beginning was actually very relaxed and informative. We were taught which food to forage, how to set traps and how to slaughter the animals we might catch. There is something incredibly rewarding in such activity, as though we are connecting back to our most primal way of life. I felt so content, like I was exactly where I was supposed to be in life.

When the relaxing days came to an end we were given a set of Second World War-era battledress and a greatcoat. We would be searched by the directing staff to make sure we had no bits of helpful kit in our pockets and I was feeling very clever because I'd hollowed out the heels of my boots so that I could hide some small survival tools inside. I tried not to smile when the staff gave me the all clear, but then a bored-looking medic inspected my boots and saw where I'd glued the heels back up. I wanted to shove those boots where the sun didn't shine, I can tell you!

Naturally, the course was run at a time when the weather was atrocious – pouring rain and strong winds on a good day! They wanted us rundown, knackered, and to this end we had to pass through a series of checkpoints, where we would have to meet an 'agent' who would give us our next rendezvous, the idea being to simulate that we were being passed along a network – just as my dad had done to escape the Nazi forces.

There was a hunter force on our heels as we traversed the wooded and mountainous terrain and escape was not a possibility. It was a matter of when, not if, they got you and should you happen to make it to the final RV (rendezvous), they'd snatch you there.

Once 'in the bag', as capture was known, we were stripped, blindfolded and put into a stress position, which makes your muscles burn and your limbs shake. That might be some people's idea of a good time, but not mine. White noise blasted constantly from speakers, battering eardrums and causing stress to an already fatigued mind. This went on for hours on end. Occasionally we were dragged off to be interrogated by the 'green slime', as the military intelligence types are known. They used all kinds of tricks to get you to talk, but so long as you kept your mouth shut, you'd be alright. Unfortunately, one of my close mates on the course started singing like a baby, telling them what they wanted to hear, and that was him done, no second chances.

I didn't give anything up to the interrogators. The stress positions hurt like hell, but the thought of quitting was far more painful and I'm not exaggerating when I say that I would rather have died than failed. I'd come too far and I wanted to be badged more than anything. A bull-headed approach, it was the most difficult thing I've ever put my body through, but sometimes you have to give yourself no other option but success.

And it worked. When my blindfold was pulled away and a smiling member of the directing staff (DS) offered me his hand, I knew my life was forever changed.

4

BADGED

By passing the escape and evasion phase I had overcome the last major hurdle to becoming a special forces soldier, but there was still time to mess up. In fact, even when you're finally accepted in, you remain on probation for your first nine years and can be sent back to your parent unit at any time for an unlimited number of transgressions.

Before we could join a sabre squadron, those of us who passed escape and evasion were sent to the Parachute Training School at RAF Brize Norton in Oxfordshire. The school's motto is 'Knowledge Dispels Fear', but I wasn't apprehensive at all. I'd never thrown myself out of an aircraft before but I was looking forward to the experience.

We completed eight descents, both with and without equipment, and during the night and day. Throwing yourself into a black void is daunting, but it was exactly the kind of soldiering I was looking for. There is no such thing as a graceful landing in this kind of parachuting as the circular canopies are designed to get you to the ground as quickly as possible so that the enemy can't pick you off in the sky.

Such speed and low-altitude jumps came with risk. Sadly, one of our trainees died on the course when his parachute failed to fully deploy and he 'candled', as we called it, into the ground. It was a sobering reminder that you didn't need to be at war to die in service of your country. Unfortunately, such deaths are unavoidable. Special forces work means pushing limits to find an advantage over the enemy and when working at such extremes, there will be accidents. The way I see it, the men who die in training have sacrificed themselves for their brothers just as if they had died on the battlefield.

Our jumps done, there were no more hurdles to overcome – at least for a moment. Of the hundreds who had attempted selection, 35 of us 'passed out' and were accepted into the regiment. Unlike in the army, there was no fanfare or parade. We were called into the regimental sergeant major's office one by one and when my turn came, he tossed a sand-coloured beret to me, and gave me two rules: 'No tromboning the pad wives and be there when the bell rings.' For those who don't speak fluent squaddie, that means no shagging other people's wives and always be ready when duty calls.

I was elated to receive my beret and become a special forces soldier. It was, without doubt, the proudest moment of my life. It's a great feeling to be able to look at yourself in the mirror and know that you didn't back down from the challenge you set for yourself, no matter how hard things got. I had made a promise to myself that I would become a special forces soldier.

I had my family's support, but no one else but me would have suffered if I'd quit. For the rest of my life, I would be able to look on this moment and know that I was a man of my word.

* * *

22 SAS was made up of five squadrons: A, B, D, G were full-time and L Det was a reserve unit that could be called upon in times when the regiment was overstretched. There were four troops to each squadron, each with a particular speciality: Air, Mountain, Boat, Mobility. Each troop should be made up of 16 men, but it was rarely the case that we were fully manned. This was down to having people in postings, away on courses, injuries and general attrition.

I was assigned to D Squadron, Mobility Troop, whose remit was all things vehicle. As we would operate behind enemy lines it wasn't enough for us to drive – we needed to know how to maintain and repair them, too.

Our troop leader was a massive Fijian named Hoss Lagari. As you can imagine, he was a keen rugby player. He had also been part of the SAS team arrested in Ireland after crossing the border and coming to a Garda VCP in '76 – an incident that had made the papers and set politicians off on another round of squabbling.

Sabre squadrons work on a rotation which I can't go into for reasons of operational security, but suffice to say, D Squadron was not on operations and was committed to training when

I arrived. That worked out great for me as I was sent on the highly coveted bodyguard course, which qualified me to guard VIPs up to, and including, the US President. After that plain-clothes course I was back in uniform for a communications course, which was run by a friendly instructor, Eddie Mooney. He taught us Morse code and I picked up the skill pretty quickly. Eddie was impressed and we became good mates.

Once I had the comms qualification under my belt I was sent on a patrol medic course. Again, operating behind the lines, we couldn't expect to have help from anyone but ourselves. The course was ten weeks of intensive training, including a four-week stint at St Mary's Hospital in London. I discovered that I had a real passion for medicine and actively pursued training in it for the rest of my career. As they said at Brize Norton, 'Knowledge dispels fear.' Well, that is certainly true of medical training. The biggest fear of most soldiers is – under-standably – death and injury. If you have a good medic with you, a soldier's mind can be put at ease and he can concentrate more on the job at hand. Still, I hoped that it would be my marksmanship and not my medical skills that I would soon be putting into practice.

It was time to go back over the water.

* * *

In the winter of 1979 D Squadron were deployed to Northern Ireland and Mobility Troop were assigned to County Derry.

I wasn't unhappy with my place in the troop, but at the same time, I felt like an outsider. I was the only one in Mobility who hadn't come from the Parachute Regiment, which has its own ethos and fraternity. It's not that they treated me badly, but they had years of shared experience and shared acquaintances. It would have been just the same if there was a troop full of Riflemen and only one paratrooper. To the Paras I would always be a 'hat' – the term they used for anyone outside of their regiment. Unlike the SAS, the Parachute Regiment does not have a Masonic lodge, but a clique is a clique.

Coming into selection, I'd been a full corporal but everyone reverts to trooper when they get badged. That was no problem for me as an SAS trooper makes the same money as an infantry full screw, but any rank above corporal took a pay cut when they joined the special forces. There was no special forces pay back then, nor SF pensions.

Of course, money wasn't the motivation behind joining the regiment. I had come here to soldier and I wasn't disappointed. During my Green Jacket tours of the province of Ulster I had felt like we were on the back foot, sometimes with apathetic officers. With the regiment, I felt like we were taking the fight to the enemy. Everything came together for me and I soon realised that we would never defeat PIRA by only having green units patrolling the streets. It was the secret war that would win it – a combination of intelligence gathering by Special Branch and strikes carried out by ourselves.

That didn't mean that line infantry battalions were not important, however – far from it. If we got in the shit, it would be them that acted as our Quick Reaction Force (QRF) and to that end we always had a liaison officer with them when we were carrying out operations. During this tour, it was the Royal Anglians who were operating in Derry. Another regiment with a proud and storied history, it can trace its lineage back to 1685.

On my last tour, patrolling had been done in bricks or sections. This time, I was on my own. Sometimes I'd drive, sometimes I'd walk. It was always in plain clothes and with a concealed pistol. People picture the SAS kicking in doors and though that is one part of the job, we spend a lot of our time on surveillance and intelligence gathering. I got to know every nook and cranny of Derry and when I wasn't doing that as a mobile patrol, I was lying in a hole in the ground or in an attic, scoping out people and places of interest from an Observation Post (OP).

We got very little information from the locals. This was a firmly Republican area and any 'touts', as informants were known, met a nasty end at the hands of PIRA's interrogators and enforcers. Sinn Fein's Martin McGuinness headed PIRA at the time. I was told that he'd been turned while in custody and was informing on his own side. I didn't know this for sure, but it wouldn't surprise me. A lot of our enemy were just cowards and thugs who ran extortion rackets and drugs. They were no different to any other gang and were not interested in a fight against people who could stand up to them. There were others in the terrorist ranks who truly believed in their cause and weren't afraid to scrap and these people I had respect for. It didn't mean that I liked them or that I wouldn't kill them, but if they wanted a shootout, fighter to fighter, then I could at least respect that they had some guts. After all, I wouldn't have fancied my chances going up against the SAS.

* * *

Over the water we worked with some great operators from the Royal Ulster Constabulary (RUC), both from Special Branch and the Headquarters Mobile Support Unit (HMSU) – the RUC's equivalent of the Metropolitan Police's SO19 firearms unit. HMSU would throw in the cordons around our operations and so we had to have trust in them, which we did.

Although there was always a danger on the mainland, we could still expect a break between tours. Not so for the RUC officers. Those guys lived in the province and 300 paid with their lives during the Troubles. Many were murdered in their own homes, others abducted and tortured before being executed – it was a dirty fucking war.

In August 1979, Lord Mountbatten, a hero of the Second World War and the last viceroy of India, was assassinated by the Provisional Irish Republican Army. A bomb had been placed aboard his fishing boat, *Shadow V*, in Mullaghmore, County

Sligo, and despite knowing he was accompanied by his twin grandsons, the terrorists detonated the device remotely. Mountbatten, one of his grandsons, Nicholas (14) and 15-year-old Paul Maxwell who worked on the boat were killed instantly. Another passenger, Baroness Brabourne, who was 82, died of her wounds the day after the attack. The remaining passengers, who included Mountbatten's teenage daughters, were severely injured. It was a disgusting, cowardly attack that left those of us in the regiment hungry for revenge.

And while the fresh news was still sinking in, the day wasn't even done. Later that afternoon, 18 British soldiers were killed in an IED attack at Warrenpoint. The first bomb was hidden in a hay rig at the side of the road and caused casualties, but the attack wouldn't stop there. The enemy had watched our drills and knew how the army would respond. After such attacks, an Incident Control Point (ICP) would be set up and PIRA guessed perfectly which site would be chosen. As the unit was dealing with the casualties, a second bomb detonated beside a stone wall being used as the ICP. It was bloody carnage and the worst loss of life that the British Army had suffered in a single day in over 10 years. Going forward, all soldiers would be taught to look for secondary devices after an IED attack, but it was too late for these men.

As always in war, lessons had to be bought and paid for in blood.

5

ASSASSINS

When my first child, David, came into the world in 1979, I was lying in a freezing-cold hole in the ground. I would have liked to have been there for him from the beginning, but it wouldn't have mattered if I was in the cold OP, or at the hospital.

When I had left my wife, it became very difficult to stay in contact with my boy. It was only when he was 30 years old that we would finally meet in person. I tried not to be angry about the time that had been lost and just be happy that we had met at last. I'm very grateful to have him in my life.

Marriage is hard and being married in the army is harder still. There's a lot of reasons why. Of course, there's the time away from each other, but that's not always a bad thing if a partner doesn't have a wandering eye – absence really can make the heart grow fonder.

I think the biggest issue in military marriages is that the husband and wife belong to different worlds and it's hard for one to fully understand the other. If I'm honest with myself, I don't know if I ever tried to really explain my own feelings and if I'd tried, I don't even know if I could have done so properly. Writing this book, I have the benefit of 40 years of hindsight. I've been through several more ups and downs and I've watched my children grow up. I'm not the young soldier that I was. Back then, I didn't know how to tell my wife that I felt I had been born for this life. I didn't know how to explain to her that any life other than soldiering would feel like a fate worse than death: I was who I had to be. And she had her own path. She wanted someone who would be home every night. Someone whose whereabouts she knew at all times. She wanted stability, I wanted war – the two are incompatible.

I always knew that in my gut, but again, trusting your instincts is usually something you only learn to do with experience. I had ignored my gut and listened to my ego, which had convinced me to get back with her. Ironically, it was my ego that took a beating when I had to drop out of selection. After that, I knew we were doomed. I filed for divorce shortly after, but it was another three years before I got it.

Now a single man and back from Northern Ireland, I went into Hereford with a few of the lads to drink. One of our favourite spots was the 'Ulu Bar', which was owned by an SAS veteran of the Malaya campaign.

We were a couple of pints in when I saw a beautiful blonde girl sitting on the other side of the bar. I plucked up my courage, walked across and gave her the best chat-up line I could think of: 'I'm a Green Jacket.'

'What do you want?' she said back, 'a gold star?'

Bloody hell, I knew it was a bad opening line, but I deflated immediately. Still, I hadn't passed selection by giving up easily and after a bit more work and a few drinks, she agreed to meet me for a date. Yet again, tenacity had paid off!

My new partner – Jenny – was a lot more understanding of my choice of lifestyle and accepted me for who I was, rather than being angry because I wouldn't change to what she wanted.

Not long after we started to date in 1980 I went to America on a 10-week exercise called 'Thumper's Glory'. It was a great trip with the boys, but while we were away hostages were taken at the Iranian Embassy, and the siege would become famous for the SAS's role. All of us felt very jealous watching it on TV and we'd have loved to have been there of course, but we knew we'd get our chance in due course. For now, we were very proud of the lads who conducted the rescue and of our regiment as a whole.

For the exercise we were accommodated in Fort Walton, Florida, and the sheriff came out to have a friendly chat with us. His biggest worry was drink driving and he told us to 'arrive alive'. I hadn't expected that we would have much time to get on the beers, but more fool me, as the true nature of the trip became apparent. It was our squadron commander's last days in the regiment and he wanted to go out in style – and with a suntan! Training was relaxed and we did little of it. Work hard, play harder! Don't want to go into too many details, but let's just say we left the locals in a state of shock.

Things weren't all fun and games, however. Not long after arriving, we attended a memorial service for the American servicemen killed during a failed hostage rescue in Iran. It was hard for me to believe that not long ago, Iranian soldiers had been welcome guests at our British Army shooting competition. A lot can change in a few years, especially when political leaders are involved.

At the service were the surviving members of the crew and I got a chance to talk with them. It was a deeply humbling experience and one I felt honoured to have.

On one of our many 'quiet pints' I had enough booze to loosen my tongue and I told Andy, the Air Troop sergeant, that I would like to cross deck and join them. I'd never been a petrol-head and the maintenance of vehicles was really not my thing. As well as that, as mentioned previously, Mobility consisted of mostly former Parachute Regiment guys who had their own kind of clique, which is understandable, but I felt like an outsider. The next morning, while I was brushing my teeth, Andy came in and told me to move my kit into Air Troop's accommodation.

As I moved my gear, Mobility Troop's staff sergeant gave me a stern look. I could have handled my request better, but I wasn't sorry to be moving. It wasn't like I was leaving the troop in time of war, I just wanted to find the right fit for me in the regiment and Mobility Troop wasn't it.

No sooner had I unpacked in Air Troop's accommodation than Andy told me to pack again. For a horrible moment I thought that I was going back to my old troop, but he shook his head: 'You're going on a free fall course,' he said. 'And you start today.'

*   *   *

Something very interesting occurred at the beginning of my free fall course. Our first jump wasn't from a plane at all, but a 30-foot high board and 'onto' a fan. The fan was strong enough to hold even a big bloke in the air, but for some people, jumping down towards it was too much.

An army chaplain was one such person who failed the test. He went up onto the board several times, but couldn't bring himself to do it. I wasn't a practising Christian, but I had faith from my time attending church with my parents. I wondered how strongly the padre could actually believe in God if he didn't trust him on a 30-foot drop.

The attitude of the other men was different. As we waited to go out of the back of a C-130 Hercules, I heard one of the soldiers say, 'It's better to die than not jump.' I couldn't agree with him more. The thought of not exiting the aircraft was not one that I ever entertained. Not only would my career in the regiment be over, but I wouldn't be able to look at myself in the mirror. Shame is a powerful force and a useful one. I had no problem jumping and I found that I actually loved the experience – I would go on to jump more than 800 times in the army, although one jump in Florida nearly ended that career early.

It was on my third free fall that things went badly. After exiting the aircraft, I went into a flat spin and no matter how much I arched my back into the correct position, I kept on spinning. If I couldn't get control of my descent, my parachute risked tangling when it deployed and that could send me candling into the ground with a closed canopy and I'd be the army's latest training death. At least I could see the earth below me and I decided that because I was the right way up, I had no choice but to take my chances – a tangled canopy was dangerous, no canopy was guaranteed to be fatal.

I pulled the canopy handle – hard work when you're spinning at speed – but I'd taken hold of the wrong one and deployed my reserve instead of the main. Because it's meant for emergency use closer to the ground, the reserve chute deploys a lot faster and I went from a 120mph fall to a momentary dead stop as the canopy caught air and I was snapped up in the harness – it was such a violent movement that the blood vessels in my eyes burst instantly.

Fortunately, I could still see and though a little shaken, I landed without further incident. However, with my red eyes I looked like I'd been possessed by the devil and one of the camp catering staff almost had a heart attack when she saw me:

'Holy mama!'

Are you familiar with the saying 'what goes on tour, stays on tour'? Well, one of our squadron was not. He'd been reporting back to his wife about the boozy antics of the other blokes and she in turn spread the rumours with the other pad wives (army wives). Loose lips sink ships and marriages. When we arrived back in Hereford, six of the guys returned to divorce papers. It caused such a stink that the exercise wasn't run again for another decade!

One of the lads – another Tony – was a little older than me and we'd done selection together. He met an 18-year-old American lifeguard, fell in love and bought himself out of the army so that he could move to the States. I couldn't imagine going through all of that work on selection just to buy yourself out a year later. Then again, I couldn't imagine saying goodbye to my wife and three kids for someone I'd just met, but that's what Tony did. The last I heard, he was living in Alabama and selling used cars.

Thankfully, my own relationship with Jenny was steady. So steady in fact that we tied the knot and I really enjoyed the time with her before it was time to pack the bags again – I was going back over the water for a fourth tour.

Air Troop were sent to Belfast, where we were stationed at Hollywood Barracks. Our roles were to conduct OPs, provide a QRF for shoots on the Green Army and Royal Ulster Constabulary and carry out the occasional raid. Unfortunately, Special Branch ended up moving us out of the city after another troop mistakenly shot the wrong person.

Our squadron suffered its own casualty. An assault was put in on a house on the Falls Road, where several gunmen were believed to be located. The troop's officer was the first through the door and he was shot in the head instantly from an M60 machine gun. Fortunately for the men who followed him in, the belt-fed gun – possibly supplied by sympathisers in America – only fired the one bullet before it malfunctioned, otherwise it would have been carnage. Unbeknown to the terrorists, the weapons had been found in a hide, where they had been given trackers and 'jarked' – a process that rendered the weapon totally inoperable, or only able to fire one round. Unfortunately for the brave officer, on this day it was one round too many.

The other gunmen quickly surrendered – they didn't have much guts for a fight once it was clear they'd lose it. They threw their hands up in surrender, knowing they would be taken in alive. If the shoe was on the other foot and they took us prisoner, we could expect to be tortured and executed, but our men played by the rules, even if we didn't like them – I'd be lying if I said I didn't want to kill the bastards.

I wasn't alone. One of the RUC officers who ran the show had been a source handler earlier in his career, meaning that he dealt with the touts. One had told him where he could find a cached weapon, but when the officer picked it up an explosive went off and took his eye and arm. I said it earlier in the book, but it bears repeating here: 'If you didn't put it down, don't pick it up'.

Another cold January morning, I was staking out a house in County Tyrone when we saw a massive fire on the horizon

– Norman Stronge, a senior Ulster Unionist figure, had been gunned down by PIRA in his home. They'd also murdered his 48-year-old son, James. Both men received a single shot to the head.

There's a saying that 'somewhere there's a bullet with your name on it'. Stronge had actually fought from day one on the Somme and survived a battle that claimed 300,000 lives. He was mentioned in despatches (MiD) and then was awarded a Military Cross for his actions in the war, continuing to serve on the front until 1918, when he was wounded in Belgium. Imagine coming through all of that hell, then being executed in your own home beside your son. Moments before, they'd been watching television together.

What made this assassination remarkable is that it was the first time PIRA used explosives to gain entry. The press and other books have claimed that they used grenades, but that's bollocks – a grenade doesn't work that way. This hit team used a plastic explosive charge and the big question in our mind was 'who taught them how to do it?'

And the method of entry wasn't the only skilled part of the hit. The leader of the assassins – a nasty shit by the name of Lynagh – knew that the Headquarters Mobile Support Unit (HMSU) would respond and he'd set out an ambush to greet them. For some reason, the ambush didn't involve an IED and HMSU's armoured vehicles were able to withstand the small arms from the men in camouflage fatigues and balaclavas. Some of the terrorists tried to fire through the window slits, but there was armoured glass behind them. None of the RUC officers were hurt, but the terrorists escaped.

Lynagh was always on the run and would hide south of the border unless it was time for a hit, so once he got away there was no catching him until he came back for his next attack. There was a rumour going around that he had actually spent some time in the Parachute Regiment. I looked into it and didn't find anything concrete. Maybe it was total bollocks, or perhaps someone had erased that part of history.

The question of who had taught PIRA explosive entry was not one that was ever answered, at least not to my ears. Maybe someone in the Irish military. Maybe a mercenary. Maybe an American veteran sympathiser. A lot of PIRA's money came from America in support of their war. Weapons, too. I'm sure that from a distance the terrorists looked like noble heroes to them, but the reality of what terrorism is struck America in 2001. Perhaps if that terrible day had occurred a few decades earlier, people wouldn't have been putting their hands in their pockets to support an organisation that routinely – and deliberately – detonated bombs that killed and maimed ordinary men, women and children.

I'm glad to say Lynagh's luck ran out in 1987. With seven accomplices, he was on his way to attack an RUC station when they drove into an ambush.

All eight terrorists were killed.

It was a good day for the SAS.

* * *

Things can change quickly on tour and one day, myself and two other operators were re-tasked to go to the home of Bernadette Devlin, a Republican agitator with no love for the British soldier. Still, when we were told that there was a credible threat on her life from loyalists, it was up to us to put our lives on the line to protect her – funny how that works, isn't it?

We were given a six-figure grid reference and arrived just as dawn was breaking. Our plan was to find an OP where we could watch her house and respond quickly to threats, but moments after we arrived, a car stopped outside of her house and three armed men got out, broke down the door and started shooting.

There was no time for us to do anything other than sprint towards the house, weapons in hand. After outrunning the others, I arrived just as the assassins were leaving the house. I pulled my M16 up into the aim. The first terrorist had a pistol in his hand and I had him dead to rights. If I pulled the trigger, it would be a justified killing and he stared back at me in total shock. I took up the trigger's slack. He quickly decided that he didn't want to die and dropped his pistol onto the frosted ground. The other two assassins quickly followed suit.

'Get against the fucking wall!' I told them.

'Which way's the wall?' One of the men's balaclavas had slipped down over his eyes, so I gave him a friendly shove to aid his sense of direction.

Entering the house, I found a man leaning up against a wall, bright red arterial blood pumping from a wound in his arm. Kids were wailing. Entering a bedroom, I found Devlin lying naked on the floor, bloodied from five gunshot wounds. She'd been in bed when the gunmen entered the house and had quickly rolled onto the floor – the mattress saved her life. Devlin was surrounded by her three whimpering kids. They were understandably shaken, but one of them still managed to look at me with utter hatred in her eyes. I wasn't surprised when years later she was convicted of bombing a British Army barracks in Germany.

When the assassins had arrived on the scene we had sent a contact report out, but couldn't follow it up due to the radio battery dying, as they often did in the cold. We had no way of knowing if the report had been received – the assassins had ripped the landline wiring out. Being the fastest out of the three of us, I sprinted across the snow-covered fields to the nearest house. From there I called in to the squadron at Portadown.

'Is she alive?' the officer commanding asked.

'Yes, boss, but I don't think she will be for long.'

By the time that I ran back to the Devlin house, soldiers from the Parachute Regiment had arrived – they'd heard our contact report before the radio died.

Special Branch arrived to take the three assassins away and a helicopter came to rush Devlin and her husband to hospital. Both survived and as you can imagine, they were very grateful to the SAS.

Ha! Not one bit of it. Devlin hated us and said that we had deliberately delayed intervening and coming to the rescue. Next time she can run across the fields herself, the ungrateful bugger!

As you can imagine, there was a mixed reaction to SAS soldiers saving the life of someone who – quite frankly – wanted us dead. Still, we had acted within the rules of engagement and law and I had no compunction about our actions. For those who say we delayed, I ask you this: if we wanted her dead, we could have waited until she had expired before going for help. We could even have sent the assassins back into the house. Of course, I'm wasting my breath. People have this idea in their heads that the SAS were in the province as assassins ourselves, but the truth was we very rarely pulled the trigger. We knew all the players and where they lived. If 'shoot to kill' was real, we could have emptied the province of terrorists in a week.

The three would-be assassins received 15 years each for attempted murder, which seems a light sentence, all things considered. I had wondered where we got the first news that they were to make an attempt on Devlin's life and I got my answer soon enough. A loyalist commander had sold them out in return for a new life in the States – what a game we pawns play!

* * *

After a cold winter in the province I was excited to hear that D Squadron were going to Greece for a six-week trip. The rumour was it would be one of those exercises that was a real swan in the park, with plenty of time on the beach and in the bars, so you can imagine my delight when I was told that I would be staying in the UK to go to Brecon instead!

The moorland and mountainsides of South Wales have their charms, but they don't look quite so pretty when you're crawling up freezing-cold streams and lying in muddy ditches. Soon I would be doing plenty of both because I was being sent back to the Infantry Battle School to attend Senior Brecon. This was the course attended by all full corporals who wanted to progress to sergeants in infantry regiments, including the special forces. Obviously, coming from the SAS, I would be flying the flag for the regiment and couldn't afford to be anything other than on top of my soldiering game – regimental pride was at stake.

Not wanting to miss out on the trip to Greece, I questioned why I was going on seniors so early in my SAS career. I was told that it was to keep me on the promotion ladder in my parent regiment and that shut me up quickly enough: it was a stark reminder that you are on probation for the first nine years of your special forces career. You can be Returned To Unit (RTU'd) at any time, for any number of reasons. After the nine-year point you were accepted onto the permanent cadre and usually expected to see out the rest of your career in the special forces world. In other words, for career purposes, you belong to the SAS – fair enough considering how much money and training they have pumped into you after almost a decade of service. I never asked what happens if there were grounds for dismissal after the nine-year point. Some things are best left unknown! If I had to guess, I'd say it probably ends in a very dull and unglamorous posting to a firing range on the other side of the world.

Sennybridge Training Area (SENTA) is a pretty bleak and desolate landscape, one of those places where you can somehow go through all four seasons of weather inside an hour! It tends to be on the wet side, but no one joins the infantry and expects to stay warm and dry. Almost 40 years later, I'd see a meme going round the internet with a picture of a British weather forecast – suns all over the country but a raincloud over Senny-bridge. That sums it up!

To be eligible to attend Senior Brecon you must complete Junior Brecon, which I had done in 1976 just after I got married. Jenny didn't mind that I was going away – she understood who I was, and that to be happy I had to be soldiering, and making the most of my career. Leopard-crawling through streams isn't everyone's idea of a honeymoon, but I must say I enjoyed the experience overall. Very few people actually enjoy being cold, wet and tired, but there's a tremendous sense of satisfaction in feeling that way and cracking on anyway, not to mention the adrenaline rush that comes from a well-executed section attack using live grenades and ammunition.

That being said, in 1981 I would rather have been sitting on a beach in Greece, but the army has long since laughed at the desires of mortal men! But I was cheered to know that I would be joined by my mate Paul Bunker. Seniors and Juniors run concurrently, and because Paul had come to the SAS from the non-infantry unit, he never had a chance to attend the courses before and was required to get it under his belt. This occurred quite a lot in the regiment as there were plenty of people who passed selection that weren't from an infantry background. I believe that we had – and still have – the finest infantry in the world and that starts with good training at places like Sennybridge. Special forces work is the basics done well and there's nowhere better to master the mechanics of front-line work than the Infantry Battle School. As we would soon see, this focus on section-level tactics would pay dividends for the British Army.

I spent a lot of time with Paul on the course, mostly in the downtime between lessons and exercises. I also knew some of the instructors at the school, who had come from 2 RGJ, including Pete Hopkins, who had been one of my instructors during the 'cadre from hell'. There's just no escaping some people! But in all honesty, you wouldn't want to escape Pete, not when it came to learning your trade. He was an excellent instructor and I learned a lot about soldiering from him.

All of the instructors were senior NCOs and they were just as professional and switched-on as Pete. One of them was a Para called Dave Fenwick, who would soon become infamous for going AWOL from Brecon. He didn't do so to avoid soldiering, but to get more of it! Dave stowed away on board one of the ships bound for the Falklands, evading all searches and not revealing himself until the ships were too far to send him back – now there's a man born for war! You've probably seen pictures of him as it was he who was photographed raising the British flag at the Governor's office at the end of the war. For some reason, credit was given to the Royal Marines. Perhaps it was because they wanted to restore honour for events that would transpire at the beginning of the war, not that I feel there was honour to be restored. Regardless, if you want to start an argument between a Para and a Bootneck, ask who raised the flag over Port Stanley. And if you want to start a fight between a Para and Rifleman, ask who took Pegasus Bridge!

There was plenty of regimental rivalry at Brecon and to be honest, I loved it. Not only did it make for good banter – essential when you're cold, wet and tired – but it was a connection to those who had gone before us. The last survivor of the Napoleonic campaigns died long before I was born, but I was still proud of them and what they achieved. Every regiment has its special days, whether Minden Day for the Princess of Wales's Royal Regiment, Arnhem Day for the Paras or Rorke's Drift Day for the Royal Welsh.

Just as we had in basic training and every other cadre, we worked in three sections making up the platoon (sometimes referred to as a 'syndicate' on the course). My section had the 'good luck' to have an instructor from the Royal Regiment of Fusiliers. Like a lot of other soldiers, he had passed SAS selection in the Navy, Army and Air Force Institutes (NAAFI) – meaning he could talk a good game over a beer, but he was never actually badged. The fact that I was actually in the regiment made the power dynamic between us a bit strange. He was my instructor and there were definitely things that I could learn from him, but I had passed into a level of soldiering that he had not and I think that bothered him.

Thankfully, there was someone in my section who used to regularly draw the attention away from me and we became good pals. Dick Catton was a mortarman from 1 Para. Tall, gangly and blond, he looked like he'd just stepped off a Viking longship and lived up to his ancestors' reputations when it came to being a nightmare on the ale and a general social hand grenade. Like the rest of 1 Para, Dick would be gutted not to get down to the Falklands the year after we finished the course. We kept in touch as I was always hopeful that he would turn up badged at Hereford one day, but it didn't happen.

Overall, I enjoyed Seniors and passed without incident. The closest my instructor ever got to Hereford was in his head and he left the army in explosive fashion: while returning to his parent unit based across the water in Northern Ireland, he was found to have explosives in his possession. I'm assuming he'd taken these from Brecon and for what reason, your guess is as good as mine. He was court-martialled, but I didn't ever learn the sentence. I'd be surprised if it didn't send him back to Civvy Street, though. Whatever, it wasn't my worry. In fact, things were looking up for me and I was finally going someplace hot and sunny.

* * *

Later in 1981, D Squadron deployed to Kenya, where we stayed on a farm belonging to an expat and practised our drills on C130s and Scout helicopters.

One day I was 'fined' by an NCO for not putting my shirt on before dismounting a truck, the price of which was a couple of slabs of beer. I was more than happy to oblige as it was my birthday, but a jovial time soon turned sour. One of the experienced blokes, Scobie, began berating the squadron commander for his conduct at the battle of Operation Storm – a battle in Oman, where every soldier in the nine-man patrol had been wounded and the officer had been relieved of command by Peter de la Billière, the brigadier running special forces. For this outburst Scobie was 'fined' and ordered to replenish our supply of beers. Everyone made mistakes in camp or on exercise and the system of fining was a fun way to get the beers in. Of course, we'd often try and stitch each other up and it was that kind of banter that made the squadron such a great place to be. We were young, with good mates and plenty of excitement – what a life!

* * *

There's a lot of ways to snuff it in the army and I almost came a cropper in the Kenyan bush. We were operating on the slopes of Mount Kenya and realised we'd set up camp at an elephant watering hole. Not wanting to get crushed in our sleep, we took to the trees and slept in the branches. I imagine this was how mankind used to do it in the early days and no one fell out!

The next day I was patrol scout and leading us through thick brush. I came to a pile of elephant shit and stopped to pick up a piece. My patrol commander asked me to guess how fresh the dung was, but before I could reply a massive bull elephant lunged towards me from behind a thick patch of bamboo! Fortunately, the bamboo thicket was strong enough to hold him back, else I would have been trampled to death. Our patrol had practised for contact front, left, right and rear, but never 'Contact, elephant!' and so we went scurrying in all directions. Once we finally reassembled, I looked at the patrol commander and said: 'I think the dung was pretty fresh.'

Not satisfied with just risking death by elephant, we began parachuting by jumping from the Scout helicopter. During this time I became very friendly with the heli's crewman, Johno, and we remain friends to this day – I'm even a godparent to one of his children.

As is often the case when on exercise in sunny places we were visited by the regimental sergeant major (RSM), who wanted to get in on the action himself. Unfortunately, he had little experience on the the kind of parachute we were using and collided with another jumper mid-air. The RSM hit the ground hard and was busted up in a bad way. I put my medical training to use and patched him up as best as I could, then we loaded him onto the heli so that he could be flown to the hospital in Nairobi. He recovered from the accident, but didn't jump much after that! Eventually, when he retired, this former RSM of the SAS would become a range warden at Hereford. To me, that seemed like a massive step down, but he seemed happy enough – each to their own.

After the heli jumps we conducted live firing exercises at Archer's Post – known as 'Archer's Roast' to the troops for its proximity to the equator and subsequent red-hot temperature. This land had been taken from the Masai tribe, who were later successful in suing the Ministry of Defence. Unfortunately, from what I saw and was told on later trips to Kenya, the millions they received in compensation seemed to be frittered away, including on expensive mobile phones (in an area with little to no signal), convertible cars and other trinkets that did little to improve their quality of life. It seemed a real shame and I wondered who had given them such bad advice.

Our final exercise involved a static line jump out of a C-130, but due to the hard ground – dotted with trees and rocks – a third of the squadron were injured on this infiltration phase, including the officer commanding (OC). For the rest of the week, he walked wide-legged and crab-like. Not fun for him, I'm sure, but it got a laugh out of the rest of us.

This OC had replaced Mike Keely, who was well known for his part in the regiment's battle at Mirbat on 19 July 1972, which was a drawn-out fight between a small SAS team and over two hundred enemy irregulars. Wanting to prove that he still belonged on the fighting edge, Mike had gone to the Brecon Beacons to re-do the endurance march section of selection. Tragically, he developed hypothermia on the mountains. He was found by a trainee who tried to keep him warm, but died in the hills. As if that wasn't hard enough on the trainee who found him, the man was then RTU'd because he hadn't completed the march in the allotted time – no one said life in the army is fair.

Before we returned to the UK, we visited the port of Mombasa for some R&R. There is a large Islamic population in the city, but this was no issue to us at the time and we enjoyed the beach and the bars. Thirty years later, a lot of radicalisation has happened among the young men there and the Foreign & Commonwealth Office (FCO) advise against any kind of travel to the city – grenade attacks became a particularly favourite tactic of the terrorists. There have also been several attacks on shopping centres in Kenya and by good fortune, an SAS soldier was on hand on two occasions to aid with evacuating civilians to safety.

As we were about to find out, you never really know when duty will call.

6

THE CALM

Britain has never been short of enemies. We live a mostly peaceful life now, so perhaps it's not something that most people think about, but our country is a warlike nation. You don't build an empire without shedding blood and you don't hold an empire without a firm hand. Other nations greedily eye up what you've got and fancy it for themselves. It's human nature on a grand scale and I'd had a little taste of it in Gibraltar, when we garrisoned that strategic rock to keep the Spanish from seizing it – not that I ever expected them to try.

In 1982 Britain had a dirty war on its hands in Northern Ireland, but we still had a massive presence in the British Army of the Rhine (BAOR). This force was made up of tanks, artillery and infantry, and if Britain was to go into a conventional war in the eighties, I always expected it would be in Europe and against the Soviet foe.

I was wrong.

On 2 April 1982, Argentinian forces invaded and captured two small islands in the South Atlantic Ocean, including the tiny garrison of Royal Marines, who were ordered to stand down by the island's civilian leadership. If it hadn't been for this action, neither you nor I would probably ever have heard about the Falkland Islands.

Unbeknown to me and almost everyone else in the world, Argentina had disputed Britain's claim to these islands for years, despite them having been in British control for more than two centuries and the population overwhelmingly pledging allegiance to Great Britain.

Well, you can always trust a politician to disregard public opinion and in 1982, Argentina's leader did just that – no surprise from a general who had overthrown his own government in a military coup. With growing public dissent and massive inflation in his own country, General Leopoldo Galtieri needed something to divert attention from the failing economy and so he turned to that time-honoured distraction – war. When the news reached Hereford we were soon stood to (made ready for action), all of us under the mistaken impression that the Falklands were somewhere off the coast of Scotland. I couldn't understand what Argentina would want with them, or how they got north without us knowing! The Royal Marines based on the islands had put up some resistance before being told to stand down and I could only imagine how gutted they must be.

The night the news broke, my mother-in-law invited Jenny and I over for dinner. We had Pease pudding sandwiches, my favourite Northern dish. While the ladies were not ecstatic about the news of war, they were not worried either – I think we all thought that it would blow over soon and without any more violence.

For the next few days the squadrons prepared our weapons and gear for transport. It turned out my geography was wrong – *very* wrong – and rather than taking the short trip to Scotland, we were in fact gearing up for an 8,000-mile journey that would take us down both of the world's hemispheres – we would be going almost all the way to the Antarctic!

Guessing we'd probably be on the cold side – it was winter in the southern hemisphere – we went to the local sports stores looking for whatever clothing and equipment we might find to give us an edge, but there wasn't much to be had. In the early eighties, uniform and clothing was closer to what was available in the Second World War than the incredible garments available now.

It would have been nice to get specific reports on the seasons and weather on the islands – there was no internet back then for us to do our own research – but our military intelligence came up short and all we had to go on was guesswork. Unfortunately, this theme seemed to continue throughout the war. Having worked with the elite Special Branch and seen intelligence work done very well, I was extremely disappointed in our own 'green slime' in the build-up to this fight. Any information we needed we'd have to find out for ourselves.

On 4 April, we were pulled in for a briefing in the regimental theatre, known as the 'Blue Room', and there was a buzz of excitement in the air. None of us could quite believe that this would come down to a shooting war, but that didn't mean that we weren't crossing our fingers – after all, none of us had joined the SAS for peace and quiet.

Perhaps it was a sign of what was to come when the brigadier entered the room wearing his pullover back to front – it's hard to trust the man in command when he doesn't know which side of a jumper is which. After telling us that we should keep our loads on the islands under 40lb – necessity would dictate that we carried more than 100lb apiece – he began to brief us on each squadron's mission.

B Squadron had gotten the short straw, at least in terms of their chances of survival – if you wanted medals and glory, then a 'suicide mission' was the place to get it!

There was no other way to retake the island than an amphibious assault (landing from the sea) and the biggest threat to that was the enemy's Super Etendard fighters and their Exocet missiles, both of which had been supplied to Argentina by our supposed allies, the French. Nothing says 'thanks for saving us from the Nazis' quite like helping to kill our men and sink our ships.

There was no reason that Argentina would need Exocets for anything other than fighting a maritime force like Britain. France had not only armed them knowing this, but their arms company technicians continued to work on the missiles and fighters during the war – there was a direct French hand in the deaths on HMS *Sheffield* and the *Atlantic Conveyor*. Arms companies from our ally supported our enemy, but I'm not naive enough to think that British companies haven't done the same when France has been at war. As the band Ocean Colour Scene put it, 'there's no profit in peace.'

The French-built Super Etendards were at an airbase in Tierra del Fuego, the southern tip of the Argentine mainland, and B Squadron's 'suicide mission' was to land there, assault the base and destroy the aircraft. No doubt they would save many lives in the fleet by doing so, but it would likely come at the cost of their own.

After the briefing, B Company's officer commanding (OC) and a troop sergeant spoke to the regimental HQ and refused to go on the mission. My belief is that they did so to save the lives of their men and to force the higher-ups to consider a different plan. You don't become a special forces soldier without showing guts and I find it hard to believe they made their decision purely out of self-preservation. Whatever their reason, both were sacked and returned to their original units.

Having received a new OC and troop sergeant, B Squadron, Air Troop of G Squadron and one SF C130 Hercules flew to the Ascension Islands in the Atlantic. This would be the launch point for their attack on Tierra del Fuego and it would be a one-way trip. Should they survive the assault on the airbase, the men would be expected to evade capture until the war was over.

Only Margaret Thatcher – the British Prime Minister – could launch the raid. She did so several times, though it was always called off before the aircraft passed the point of no return. But this yo-yo proved too much for the C130's pilot and he suffered a nervous breakdown. We didn't talk much about mental health problems back then, but no one was under the illusion that they didn't exist.

None of us wanted to lose a squadron's worth of comrades and we were relieved when the mission was cancelled indefinitely. The reason was that the plane, a Hercules, would probably run out of fuel before reaching the target, where the plan was for it to crash land on the runway so that the troopers could disembark and attack the enemy aircraft. I thought back to the American C130 crew members I had met in Florida, who had survived their own disaster in Iran, and I was very glad that my mates would not be going into battle without a fighting chance.

* * *

Although our brigadier seemed to struggle with wool jumpers, not all Ruperts are alike and I had full confidence in the officers of our squadron. The OC and the troop commanders all had infantry backgrounds and were reasonably well experienced. Like most of us, they had served in Northern Ireland but none had taken part in the regiment's campaigns in the jungle and desert. Like me, this would be their first deployment outside of the 'dirty' war in the province. I have worked with several who were excellent soldiers and leaders. Some went on to be incredibly senior leaders, including one who reached the pinnacle to become the head of the army.

The regiment selects its officers in a process called 'Officers Week' – part of the overall selection process, where they have to pass the hills, jungle and other phases the same as an enlisted soldier does. Those who make the cut are given command of a troop for three years and if they have any sense they'll let the troop run itself. Every man who passes selection is an alpha male and not many take kindly to being micromanaged. Respect needs to go both ways and an officer will be referred to as 'Boss' rather than 'Sir'. There is no man more experienced in a troop than the staff sergeant and when there is good chemistry between him and the boss, things run very smoothly indeed.

Some enlisted men are selected from the rank to take commissions, but they're then put into roles that are non-operational, such as the training wing. Some Senior Non Commissioned Officers (SNCOs) get stars in their eyes and sell out in the name of ambition and I saw this myself when I later became part of the training wing. Even though we didn't feel like they met the grade, the regimental sergeant major (RSM) wanted us to pass several extra recruits out of the jungle – I imagine he was under pressure to meet a quota or something along those lines. Whatever the reason, all of us on the training team said that we'd walk out if men were passed against our wishes. It was up to us to ensure that only the best would be badged – people's lives depended on it. Eventually the RSM backed down and the incident didn't seem to hurt his career – he would retire as a lieutenant colonel.

* * *

A few days after the Argentinian invasion, I packed my personal belongings and prepared to spend one last night with my wife. As well as my issued gear, I'd bought a waterproof bivvy bag from a camping shop. I also had a Walkman, but for some reason, only one cassette! It was by Christopher Cross and I'd listen to it in the helicopter whenever we were on our way into a mission.

There were no tears or theatrics on my last night at home. I knew with absolute certainty that I'd be coming back and so did Jenny. We went to the pub, had a few pints with mates and I had no trouble falling asleep. I was excited, I was content and truth be told, I still thought I'd end up disappointed and the politicians would make peace before I could get anywhere near an enemy soldier.

How wrong I was.

The next day at camp, not everyone looked as excited to be going to war as I was – I'd later find out from one of those widowed by the Falklands War that her husband was certain that he wouldn't come back. I've always been an optimist myself, but you've got to respect a bloke who thinks he's heading to certain death and goes anyway. It's not like we would have dragged people onto the aircraft if they had refused to soldier – better to be short-handed than have someone who doesn't want to be there.

We left without fanfare for the air force base and on the coach talked over the latest news: Argentina were reinforcing both East and West Falkland and they had also taken South Georgia. No one in the world seemed to believe that Britain would respond militarily and the consensus was that some kind of peace would be made.

Guess again, mate.

We learned a bit more about the Royal Marines who had been stationed at Port Stanley when the Argentinian military showed up. Despite being few in number, the Bootnecks did themselves proud and put up a fierce resistance, seeing off the invading enemy, who couldn't make ground against the Royal Marines' fire. It was the islands' governor, Rex Hunt, who ordered the Bootnecks to surrender and I think this was the right decision – there was nothing to be gained by the men fighting to the death. Of course, there were plenty of armchair warriors in the UK who saw the photo of the surrender and called the Marines cowards. Well, if they felt that way, they could go down to the Falklands and show them how it's done. It's always the people who don't have to fight who are the loudest about how hard they *would* fight.

Thankfully, in recent years, several of those Royal Marines have written accounts telling their side of the story. In short, they beat back an enemy despite being vastly outnumbered and fighting with limited arms and equipment. That didn't mean that I would pass up a chance to take the piss, however!

Years later, when I was instructing a lesson on the stages of capture, I asked the class how many Bootnecks we had in the room. A few hands went up and I went to the next slide on the projector – a photo of their surrender in Port Stanley. They saw the funny side, of course. If you can't handle banter, then you definitely won't deal well with some of the real parts of war!

I didn't worry that such a thing might happen to me. As I said, I still didn't expect that we would even get to face the enemy, and if we did? I was one of the most highly trained soldiers in the world and I was deploying with an entire squadron of men who were, like me, born for war.

The only thing I feared was missing out on the fight.

* * *

Ascension Island is a small volcanic island in the South Atlantic Ocean, sitting pretty much bang in the middle between the Horn of Africa and South America. Over the past century, it had been an important coal stop for ships and a refuelling point for aircraft. Now, it was a staging post for the British military as we made our way across the hemispheres and to the Falkland Islands.

There was an RAF base on the island, which of course meant there was a place to drink and we took advantage of that in the evenings after we spent our days acclimatising and testing weapons. There was a real buzz of excitement in the air as units of all three services began to congregate at Ascension. It had been decades since Britain had put together a task force to fight a hot war and already ships were gathering at anchor off the island.

I met a crew-member from one of these vessels in a bar. I felt a tap on my shoulder and turned my head but I didn't see anyone until I looked down. There was a very short man wearing a vest and cut-off Levis with a heart stitched over the crotch. He asked for my name, so I gave him the name of my hated adversary in the troop – hopefully, he'd come asking at the squadron for him in the middle of the night.

When we were finally accommodated on a ship, we found an area to work out in the sunshine until the captain came over the tannoy: 'Would the army please put their clothes back on, you're distracting my sailors.'

Well, each to their own. They were bloody good at their jobs, and that's all that mattered to me.

While there were already several of Her Majesty's ships at anchor, the SAS were well ahead of the bulk of the army – which, of course, is part of the point of special forces. Surveillance was part of our bread and butter and to this end we put in extra lessons on the radios – it's pointless gathering intelligence if you can't pass it back! To this end, we used the PRC 319 radio, which is a big cumbersome thing, but it worked well and that's what mattered.

I called home to Jenny now and then just to chat about the usual married couple's stuff, like home life, friends, and bills – they don't stop just because you're at war! She was great with dealing with things like that and didn't ever get in a flap about me being away.

My mum wasn't quite so calm, bless her. Every time there was footage of troops on the TV, she would call Jenny, convinced she'd seen me. I didn't know any of this and Jenny did a great job of keeping Mum's feet on the ground – she was a hero of the home front.

A lot of the news contained quotes and speeches from Margaret Thatcher – otherwise known as the Iron Lady, a nickname given to her by a Soviet journalist. Quite a compliment in my book! I'd never been much involved in politics and I wasn't someone who voted. My dad was Labour through and through, but I'd never seen much difference between the parties. When it came to dinner with my wife's mining family, though, I always played the part of a Conservative supporter – anything for a bit of banter!

I didn't have a high opinion of politicians, but Thatcher was different. In a time where Britain's power was clearly on the wane, I felt she gave the country an injection of energy. Many would disagree – my wife included – but as I say, I don't think there's much difference between the parties and certain things at home would have happened under anyone's watch. What I do believe is that had Thatcher not been prime minister, we would have made a lot of noise but probably let the Falkland Islands go without a fight. Back in April 1982, while we waited in Ascension to be assigned to a vessel, I still believed that we would go home without firing a shot.

C130 traffic was increasing on the island, the flights bringing in more personnel and equipment. When we left the UK, there had been no decision on whether or not Britain would retake the islands – I say 'retake' and not 'attempt to retake' because there was no doubt in our minds that we would be successful if ordered forwards. Now the British government had stated publicly that we would use force to evict the Argentinian squatters. That didn't mean that violence was imminent, but it certainly made it more likely.

It would take boots on the ground and bayonets on the ends of rifles to evict the Argentinians from their positions and an armada was forming to carry them. 3 Commando Brigade, consisting of 41, 42 and 45 Commando, formed a large part of Operation Corporate, as the mission to liberate the islands was now known. The army was represented by 2 and 3 Para, 1/7th Gurkha Rifles, the Welsh Guards and the Scots Guards. I can only imagine how gutted the other battalions must have been back in the UK and Germany – the Falklands was shaping up to be a true infantryman's war.

In 1979, the Royal Navy had decommissioned HMS *Ark Royal*, a traditional aircraft carrier that carried a combination of 38 F4 Phantom Fighters and Buccaneer ground attack aircraft. It was a formidable platform for projecting power and I began to wonder if Argentina's junta would have invaded if it was still in service. Still, we had HMS *Hermes* and HMS *Illustrious*, both carrying Sea Harriers of the Fleet Air Arm and bolstered by Harrier GR3s of the Royal Air Force. Both carriers also held a complement of helicopters, which could also operate from the decks of the amphibious assault ships HMS *Intrepid* and HMS *Fearless* – the latter of which would operate as the task force's flagship and headquarters.

Carriers needed to be protected and to that end more than 20 other warships would converge on the Falklands, ranging from destroyers to submarines. Of course, none of this naval power would matter if we couldn't dig the enemy out of their fighting positions and a host of Royal Field Artillery (RFA) vessels gathered to transport supplies and the men who would get their boots muddy.

We were to board one such vessel, the RFA *Fort Austin*. It was carrying ammunition to the war and without the hard work and bravery of such crews, the war would never have been fought. Just as their forebears had done in the Second World War, the RFA and the Merchant Navy showed their mettle.

Being at sea wasn't really for me. That's not to say I got sick, but I would rather have hills or towns to range than any ocean. Still, I was in a good mood because of where we were going and there was an excited energy to the training that we conducted on board the *Fort Austin*, keeping our drills fresh and our bodies prepared.

Our ship would be a sitting duck for Argentinian aircraft, so it was a relief when we were joined by the destroyer HMS *Antrim*, which had been on duties in the Med before being re-routed to the war – I hoped they'd packed some warm clothes!

From the pieces of information we were given, we were hopeful our D Squadron would become the first British boots to land on the island. However, that honour would eventually go to G Squadron – they'd act as the reconnaissance squadron, operating from the carrier HMS *Hermes*.

At the time, we were kept in the dark as to what the mission of the other squadrons might be. Of course, we spent a lot of time talking about it and giving it our best guess. The general consensus was that we would be used for gathering intelligence on the enemy before the main force landed and we hoped that we would also be used to directly attack the enemy's air power ability. None of us liked the idea that the enemy could sink us before we set foot on dry land and life always feels better when you're on the offensive. After all, 'He who dares, wins'.

You make your own fun at sea and fortunately for us, HMS *Antrim* had a Lynx helicopter on its back deck. After we asked very nicely, the fleet air arm agreed to fly up so that we could make a free fall descent from the heli. It wasn't just a jolly, though, as parachuting into water is a very difficult and important skill, one that we were aware we might need to use in the dangerous waters off the islands. We didn't know what we would be doing on the campaign, but skills needed to be kept sharp – it was just all the better if practising those skills happened to be a lot of fun.

At 6,000 feet we jumped from the Lynx and deployed our canopies after a few seconds of descent. Our drop zone had been marked by flares and as I steered my chute towards it, I suddenly saw two huge shapes beneath the water. At first I thought they must be submarines, but to my delight, I realised that I was looking at a pair of blue whales! It was incredible to see and my guess is that the gentle giants had been drawn to the vibration of the ships.

After staying in the air for as long as possible to take in the breathtaking sight, we landed in a tight group on the opposite side of the ship and waited for the safety boat to pick us up. We were somewhere in the middle of the South Atlantic at the time and I reckon we must have broken the world record for furthest parachute descent from land – what a day!

D Squadron were cross-decked from RFA *Fort Austin* to HMS *Antrim*, meaning we were moved from one ship to the other – in this instance via helicopter. Space was at a premium, but it is a skill of a soldier to be able to sleep anywhere and I was comfortable enough in my sleeping bag set against a bulkhead.

Not everyone was as happy. The crew of the *Antrim* were about to start a period of leave when war broke out and many of them were pissed off about having to go to the Falklands. I just couldn't understand that mentality: you joined the Royal Navy and now there's a war, you want to go home? What kind of attitude is that?

One day the crew of the warship were running drills on their 2.4-inch guns. There was an almighty crash, but what we assumed was an accident turned out to be wilful sabotage – unhappy they weren't going home, some of the sailors had manufactured the incident so that the gun barrel fell from its mount. In all of my time in the military it was one of the most disgraceful things that I ever saw and the general consensus in the squadron was that they should be thrown overboard. If you don't want to go to war, don't join the military!

It was a sad state of affairs and not one that could last. Like it or not, the crew of the *Antrim* were going to the fight.

As a Green Jacket, my scope of the military had been pretty limited. An infantry battalion is its own ecosystem. Aside from postings – say, to a training establishment – most of an infantry soldier's career took place in the same unit, which back then consisted of 650 men. You could spend 22 years in the battalion, learning the ins and outs of your regiment intimately, but leave the army knowing little about the wider armed forces. In the SAS, your knowledge begins to expand as you work alongside men from different cap badges, but even there,

about 75 per cent of the blokes came from an infantry background. Exercises help to broaden the horizon, but nothing
had opened my eyes to the cooperation and codependence
of the three services quite like the journey south to the Falklands. The army were transported by the RFA, the RFA were
guarded by the Royal Navy, while the RAF flew top cover for
all. Winning back the islands would take the best that all the
services could provide and our first real chance to prove our
mettle was fast approaching.

One day we were buzzed by an RAF Nimrod – meaning
that it flew low and close to the *Antrim*. The Nimrod was a
beautiful aircraft – about twice the length of the Lancasters
that my father had flown in – and was proving invaluable at
this early stage of the campaign. The surveillance aircraft had
begun to arrive at Ascension on 5 April and from there they
were providing valuable top cover (patrols and reconnaissance)
for the maritime vessels – something that those of us aboard
were very grateful for. The Argentine navy had service vessels
as well as submarines and the thought of a watery grave was
not one an infanteer wished to contemplate!

Back on the home front, it seemed there was a good appetite
for war. The British press were in a bloodthirsty mood, as
reflected in the *Sun*'s headline: 'Stick It Up Your Junta!' Well,
for those of us who would be doing the sticking, it wasn't
quite so personal. I didn't feel there was any bubbling hatred
towards the Argentinians and at least some of the crew of the

Antrim would have been quite happy if the war was called off and they could go on the leave they had been expecting before being sent southwards. As the correspondent Max Hastings would later write: 'The distance of the impending encounter from Britain and from civilian casualties seemed to induce a reckless aversion to peace.'* Funny how that goes, isn't it? I doubt members of the British press would have been such enthusiastic cheerleaders for war had Fleet Street been in the range of Argentinian bombs, but such is life. There are two kinds of people who want war: warriors who are born for it and those who profit from a distance while never being at risk themselves. Speaking for the warriors I know – and I have met a lot in my life – the wish is always that a war will take place somewhere out of the way of civilians, who will not be harmed. Well, so far as it is possible to have a war like that, we were about to get it.

There was a reason for the Nimrod to fly out to us and buzz HMS *Antrim* – the aircraft dropped a floating canister on the ship's portside and this was promptly collected and brought on board. Those of us watching were beginning to get excited and guessed the canister could only contain one thing: secret orders that could not risk being transmitted across the airwaves and intercepted by a snooping enemy or their allies.

---

* *The Battle for the Falklands*, Max Hastings, Pan, 1983 edition, p. 134.

We weren't wrong. Later that day, D Squadron was brought together as one to receive our orders.

The British warriors and press would get their wish: it was time to retake the islands.

7

THE STORM

Operation Paraquet was the official name given to retaking the British island of South Georgia. Personally, I think they should have called it something more along the lines of Operation Sledgehammer, a nice aggressive name, but I wasn't asked for my opinion. Besides, all that mattered was that we were about to get in on the action.

D Squadron were elated, of course. It had been nice enough sitting around on deck and catching some sunshine, but we were heading south for a reason and that reason was war. Now, all we could hope was that the Argies would put up a fight for long enough so that we would be able to get stuck in.

On reflection, I imagine the decision for us to retake South Georgia first was a political one. While the British territory was no doubt under enemy occupation, it didn't appear that the island was being used as an air or naval base. If anything, it seemed as though a small Argentinian garrison had been dumped there so that a general could colour in a map – something that they enjoy doing – and perhaps they didn't expect that we would make the effort to go to an island so far removed from the Falklands. The British press wanted action and I expect that British politicians wanted to show all those involved that we were serious about taking back the islands and that we weren't afraid to get our hands bloodied.

The first recce on the island was conducted by the submarine HMS *Conqueror*, which would soon become a household name. After confirming that there was no Argentine naval presence, HMS *Conqueror* left to take up station to the northwest – a decision that would soon prove fatal for hundreds.

Originally, a company of the Royal Marines had been earmarked for the operation and landing on South Georgia, but due to the threat of Argentina's own submarines, their slower Royal Fleet Auxiliary (RFA) vessel was being held back at a distance and in deeper waters. So the job had instead been handed over to D Squadron and elements of the Special Boat Service – or 'Shakies', as we called them. I have no idea where the nickname comes from, only that it annoys the Shakies and that's good enough for me!

There was a whaling station on South Georgia and Argentinian whalers had broken the law and landed on the island in March. After seeing the majesty of the blue whales only days before I was quite happy to kick the arse of anyone who hunted those beautiful creatures, but it was actually the Argentine Commandos that we would be going against. They'd landed on 3 April 1982, and I was looking forward to testing myself against them. It's one thing to call yourself a Commando and another to act like it, and I had no doubt at all that we would be too much of a match for them.

I was happy with the force that we had at our disposal. As well as the special forces element – which would be the boots on the ground – there were three naval vessels – HMS *Antrim*, HMS *Brilliant* and HMS *Plymouth* – and helicopters that had come over from HMS *Invincible* and the RFA *Tidespring*. But before you can fix (in position) an enemy so that you can destroy him, you have to find him. We didn't know the enemy numbers, or where they were, and so recce patrols would have to be launched into the Antarctic mid-winter. We'd enjoyed the sun on the way down south, but those days were gone and now the waters were choppy and the air was icy-cold – so cold, in fact, that there were icebergs floating in the ocean. We really had come a long way from home.

I didn't want to end up in that sea and neither did our commanders. No one knew the position of the enemy submarine, the *Santa Fe*, but she was suspected to be lurking in this area. If we approached the shallow waters closer to the shore, let alone dropped anchor, the ships would be a sitting duck for the sub's deadly torpedoes.

It was decided that Mountain Troop would be airlifted onto the Fortuna Glacier so that they could then observe the settlement of Grytviken. It almost felt like we were retreading the glory days of the British Empire as this was the point where Shackleton and his crew had landed. They had required rescue when his ships became stuck in the ice and we all hoped that things would go better for Mountain Troop. The Mountain Leaders of the Royal Marines were not optimistic of this and warned against any kind of heli insertion onto the glacier, as did civilian experts who knew the terrain. Personally, I would have listened to them, but the decision wasn't mine to make. I was anxious to get ashore, but the glacier didn't sound like much fun and I was quite happy to wait for a job that would hopefully put us into direct action against the enemy.

Mountain Troop's first attempted insertion was called off because the weather was too bad to land and the Wessex helicopters returned to the ships. In the British Army, there is an attitude of 'cracking on' no matter the weather or circumstances. Combined with the 'who dares wins' mentality of the special forces, this can produce victory out of what may look like certain defeat. Unfortunately, it can also lead to bad decisions being made when the better course of action would have been to come up with another plan. SAS soldiers are strong and resilient both mentally and physically, but they are still human and subject to the same laws of nature that have killed people since the first of us walked the earth. Our equipment and helicopters were even more fallible than our men. Mountain Leaders and regional experts had warned against inserting onto the Fortuna Glacier and the pilots had turned back for a reason. I think, at this point, it was pride that was driving the decision making and sending Mountain Troop back out to try again had more to do with winning the inner battles of the officer's mess than retaking South Georgia.

'Theirs not to reason why', Mountain Troop went back out and this time the incredibly skilful helicopter crews succeeded in getting them onto the deck in one piece. It was all downhill from there and not in the good way.

Conditions were so awful that it took the patrol's scouts five hours to advance 500 metres. Icy crevasses waited to trap an unsuspecting man and the patrol's troopers were dragging sleds weighing 200lb apiece – the equivalent of another grown man. All this while snow and wind whipped with such ferocity that it was difficult to see even the soldier closest to you.

Shortly after Mountain Troop's insertion onto the glacier, a whiteout occurred. This is when the snow and wind come at such an incredible speed that the entire air seems to be white and within minutes Mountain Troop had been stripped of their tents and much of their equipment – what was supposed to be a recce patrol was now a survival situation. In that kind of cold, a man can die quickly from exposure and hypothermia.

Have you heard the expression 'things can only get better'? Well, I'm afraid that's 100 per cent false in war.

A Wessex was sent back to rescue Mountain Troop from a rapidly deteriorating situation but the winds and perilous conditions proved too much for the aircraft and it crashed onto the glacier, thankfully with no loss of life. Now the rescue crew needed to be rescued by another rescue crew.

Only they crashed, too.

It might have been funny if it wasn't so deadly. We were in danger of losing a troop and two heli crews without a shot being fired.

Their only hope was 'Humphrey', the last remaining Wessex on board the *Antrim*. If you've ever watched a penalty shootout, imagine that feeling turned up by 100,000 and that's what it was like watching Humphrey fly out to succeed where two other choppers had failed.

Mercifully, this third attempt was successful and 17 men were saved from icy graves. For his bravery and skilful flying in this and other missions, Humphrey's pilot, Ian Stanley, was awarded the Distinguished Service Order (DSO). Another of Humphrey's crew, Chris Parry, wrote about his experiences in a book called *Down South**, which I recommend. Stanley and his crew flew 17 missions into these lethal conditions, operating right on the edge of the Wessex's range. I have the greatest respect for him and his crew. Without their skill and courage it would have been a tragic day for both the SAS and the RAF.

Within 48 hours of arriving at South Georgia we were down two helicopters and still no closer to knowing the enemy's strength and dispositions. To rectify this, Boat Troop were tasked with launching a recce on Grass Island, but three of their Gemini inflatable boats broke down en route and had to be

---

* *Down South: A Falklands War Diary*, Chris Parry, 2012.

towed by the remaining two. This came as little surprise to many as for years Boat Troop had been requesting stronger outboard motors. Oh well, it's not the first time troops have gone to war without the kit they required and it won't be the last. Fighting for budget is as much a part of war as fighting the enemy, but still, an accountant's decision had almost proved fatal and Operation Paraquet was in danger of turning into a farce. Thankfully, the Boat Troop lads were a lot more resilient than their boat's engines and when they finally got ashore, they were able to gather very useful intelligence on the enemy positions.

While these events had been going on, a small group of civilians from the British Antarctic Survey were in contact with our headquarters. A plan was devised to extract them so that they could be debriefed and kept safely away from the Argie Commandos. Mobility Troop were flown out to King Edward Point, where they would rendezvous with the civilians under cover of darkness.

Unfortunately, when the civilians approached the troop, they were mistaken for the enemy and Mobility Troop opened fire. I don't know which was more embarrassing – that SAS soldiers fired at the people they had come to rescue or that they missed!

We hadn't even been at the island for three days and so far every troop in the squadron bar ours had a cock-up to its name and the banter was intense, as you can imagine. Air Troop were keen to show the others how it was done, but we were yet to be given a task.

The unseen *Santa Fe* had a lot to do with that and the submarine was the biggest factor in all decision making. The only ship in our flotilla deemed capable of escaping the sub in shallow waters was HMS *Endurance*, commanded by Captain Nick Barker. Affectionately nicknamed 'Red Plum', she was little bigger than a North Sea fishing trawler and Air Troop were transferred onto her in the hope that she could take us close to shore. There was a small helicopter deck on Red Plum, but not large enough for a Wessex, and so we were winched down one by one. On board the *Endurance*, I found a crew who were a lot different in attitude from those on the *Antrim* – the ship was small in size but large in spirit. The *Endurance*'s crew were glad to be a part of the task force and they wanted to help with the war effort however they could. To that end, they'd already taken part in a reconnaissance of Saint Andrews Bay and they were the ship that made contact with the isolated British Antarctic Survey.

Once we were all on board with our equipment, we looked for any place we could to bunk down and I found a corner in the stokers' mess within the bowels of the tiny vessel. There, I met a great bunch of blokes and they treated me with a kindness that I hoped I could repay at some point. Over the coming days we would spend a lot of time chatting around the table and as I'll explain soon, things got a little rowdy, too!

The little ship also had a little helicopter – there was a Wasp perched on the back of the vessel and mounted on its rails were two AS12 air-to-ground missiles. I wondered how useful such a small aircraft and payload would be.

I soon found out.

* * *

You have to make your chances in war and when you make them, you have to take them.

The *Santa Fe* had been keeping us at arm's length from the island, but thanks to the work of the Wasp helicopter crews, she was spotted on the surface close to South Georgia and their quick actions would turn a bad start in the campaign into the beginnings of success.

The Wasp that had spotted the *Santa Fe* dived into the attack and damaged the vessel with one of its missiles. Two other Wasp helicopters flew to the scene, including ours from the *Endurance*. Excited sailors relayed the messages heard over the radio as the fight went on out of sight.

Our Wasp came back to the ship and we could see that its two missiles were gone – they'd got in on the action! Without being told, myself and a few of the other troops helped bring up fresh missiles for the heli. We might not be able to get into the fight directly, but we wanted to do our part in sinking the sub that had been stalking us.

I didn't think for a moment about the crew of the vessel that we wanted to sink. They would have followed their orders too and following their orders could have sent me and my mates down to a watery grave. I didn't hate them for that, but nor did I think about them either, or what might happen if these missiles hit their hull. It was them or us and I had a wife to get home to.

The *Santa Fe* was badly battered and though it couldn't submerge, it didn't sink. When it was clear that she was limping into harbour and out of the fight, the helicopters knocked off their attack. It was knocked out of the war and the crew didn't have to die with their ship – a win all round.

Cheers went around the *Endurance* when we heard the news and everyone wanted to shake the returning helicopter crew's hands and hear the stories. We barely knew these people, but we were all on the same team: all British and all proud.

With the *Santa Fe* out of the way, there was nothing to hold us back from assaulting the island. We had found the enemy and they were fixed.

Now, it was time to destroy them.

* * *

Orders were given for the attack.

Originally, M Company of the Royal Marines had been earmarked for this job, but that was not to be. M Company, as well as parts of D Squadron, were being transported on RFA *Tidespring*. To avoid the threat of the *Santa Fe*, the *Tidespring* had been further out from South Georgia than the rest of our small task force and was now too far to shuttle M Company in time to be the assaulting force. Our commanders wanted to take advantage of the blow of striking the *Santa Fe* and rightly so. Momentum is vital in war and we had it. There just wasn't time to wait for the *Tidespring* to close to our position and so the men on board would miss out on the attack they had hoped to carry out. I can only imagine how gutted and frustrated they must have been as they learnt that the job had instead been passed to us.

Personally, I couldn't have been more excited. This was the moment I had been born for. For the first time since the Second World War, three British naval vessels would form up, line astern, to provide naval gunfire support (NGS), sailing into Grytviken Sound to batter the mountain above the town – the plan was to creep the fire downwards and convince the enemy it was a good idea to surrender without needing to destroy civilian property in the town in which they'd made their positions. I took a photo of the warships in this action and it's one of my most cherished possessions.

The photo was taken from the deck of HMS *Brilliant*, a Type 22 frigate onto which we were cross-decked from the *Endurance*. The crew wished us well and we wished them the same – cracking blokes that I respected for their hard work and professionalism.

Following the incident of the sabotaged gun, I had a low opinion of the crew of the HMS *Antrim*, but I'm glad to say that changed as I watched them sail into the sound. Their gunnery work was excellent and couldn't be faulted.

I was watching it from the deck of the *Brilliant* because – to our chagrin – Air Troop were the reserve for the attack. D Squadron HQ, Mobility Troop and the Shakies were putting in the attack. Still, we weren't too worried, certain that at some point we would be called forward in the helicopters so that we could do our part in dislodging the Argentine forces. After all, the enemy were Commandos!

It turns out that it's a lot easier to call yourself a Commando than embody the Commando ethos and after a shelling from our ships, and some small arms from the assault force, white flags started to fly all over the settlement – the enemy had surrendered. Ha! Those of us on *Brilliant*'s helicopter deck were livid when we got the news as that meant we'd missed out on action again, but at least we could take some solace that we had been witness to a proud moment in British military history and we took our hats off to the excellent work of the Royal Navy. As much as we would have liked to get in on the fight, it was a good day – the settlement was spared destruction, the enemy were routed and at no cost to us in British lives. An Argentinian officer complained that the Brits had just walked straight through his minefield, seemingly upset that no one had had the decency to lose a leg or two! Sorry about that, mate!

Operation Paraquet had been anything but textbook. In fact, it's fair to say that at times it felt like two people boxing with blindfolds on. I consider it a miracle that after the debacle on the glacier, the attack on the *Santa Fe*, the assault on the island and resulting walk through a minefield, there was only one fatality.

The job done, Squadron Sergeant Major Lawrence Gallagher (SAS) raised the British flag above South Georgia.

It was 25 April 1982 and the liberation of the islands had begun.

S

THE RAID

South Georgia had been retaken from the enemy. We'd travelled a long way to do this and nobody likes to go home from war without a souvenir. Air Troop hadn't been called on to and from the reserve on HMS *Brilliant*, but I had a mate in Mountain Troop who I knew from our days in the Green Jackets. Doughy and a few of his mates got into the local post office, found some stamps and postcards, and stamped them with the date of the island's liberation. He gave me a few later in the campaign and I still have them to this day.

Although the Argentinian forces had surrendered at Grytviken on the 25th, there were reports of more of their so-called 'Commandos' in Leith Harbour, a small whaling station. We sailed along the coast and the buggers surrendered as soon as they saw the warships. Their commander, Captain Astiz, who was known as the 'Blond Angel of Death', had run a prison in Argentina that tortured and killed activists opposing the military Junta. A wanted war criminal, he was implicated in the disappearance of 12 people, including a nun and two French nationals – none of them were ever seen again.

The enemy had rigged the whaling station with explosives and so they were cordially invited to remove them. I was chuffed that our commanders made this decision. Why risk our own sappers and bomb disposal crews? Their job in the campaign would be dangerous enough – and several would lay down their lives doing it.

After the explosive de-rigging was completed, on the 26 April Captain Astiz formally surrendered aboard HMS Antrim. His men were still ashore and would be guarded by M Company, Royal Marines for the duration of the war. I can only imagine how gutted they must have been to sail 8,000 miles to guard prisoners. Probably not what they had in their heads when they signed on the dotted line to be Commandos, but it was a duty that needed doing. Tough break.

Captain Astiz was short, bearded and fairly nondescript except for the fact that he looked terrified. When I saw him, he had that look on his face that said, 'shit, this is it.' It was my first time seeing the enemy up close and I wasn't impressed. Of course, I'd been told about Astiz and what he'd been accused of. It's impossible to have even a shred of respect or compassion for a man who kills civilians but throws his hands up at the first sign of a proper fight. He was everything that I despised and I'm glad to report that after the surrender was accepted, Astiz was arrested, detained and later convicted by the International Criminal Court in The Hague. In 2005, a mass grave was discovered containing the bodies of the 12 people he had tortured and killed. Astiz was sentenced to life imprisonment, to be served in Argentina.

While his men would wait out the war on South Georgia, Astiz was kept in a supply cupboard on HMS *Brilliant* and the men of D Squadron took turns guarding him. I wondered what was going through his mind in the days after capture – he must have known he was in the shit. That he chose to go meekly to jail instead of fighting shows what a pathetic coward he was. As you can tell, I really didn't like the git! None of us had any sympathy and it's fair to say that he didn't get an invite to 'the mother of all parties' that followed his surrender.

This particular ruckus took place aboard the HMS *Endurance*. The SAS bounced around a lot between different vessels in the flotilla, depending on what task was at hand, and so getting everyone back together was easily accomplished with helicopters. After the surrender, Air Troop and some of the Shakies were accommodated on Red Plum for the time being. It was nice to see her crew again and I moved myself back into my home in the stokers' mess. The crew of the *Endurance* had been good to us and now we repaid them in kind – D Squadron and the Shakies hadn't been idle in Leith and a lot of wine found its way into our possession courtesy of the Argentinian officers' supplies. We said a few toasts to Astiz and thanked him for the booze – I hope he was enjoying his supply cupboard!

Alongside the wine on the mess table were weapons, grenades and ammunition taken from the enemy. There was even a 3.5-inch rocket launcher and the Special Boat Service (SBS) lads were rattling on about how great it would look in their mess in Poole.

I had other ideas about that, though, and after a long night of drinking, I was the last man standing, so to the victor, the spoils! I took the rocket launcher and hid it away in the ship, but not for my own keeping. The next day, with a very sore head, I presented the weapon to the stokers, the engine room specialists of the *Endurance*. It was soldiers who would have the honour of fighting the enemy up close, but we never would have got here without the navy and her crews. Giving them a great souvenir was the least we could do in my opinion.

I can't say the Shakies were of the same mindset and they got quite irate when they found out that their proposed trophy was missing! They kicked up such a stink that the captain of the *Endurance* ordered it to be handed back to them, but this didn't happen and so the captain ordered the ship to be searched. I was pretty pissed off at the attitude of the Shakies and decided if they wanted to be petty, I could be more petty still.

After a chat with the stokers, we decided to dump the rocket launcher into the South Atlantic.

Good luck mounting that in your mess!

* * *

Although South Georgia was a success, D Squadron had narrowly avoided several disasters.

While Boat Troop's intelligence-gathering mission on Green Island had gone well that week, both their infiltration and exfiltration had been hard work. On the way in, the engines on three of their five boats had broken down. Now, on their extraction, two engines failed again. The currents around the islands were very strong and with such light boats the two crews were quickly pulled way off course – no laughing matter. In cold and rough conditions, they were adrift and heading towards a lingering death in the Antarctic. Fortunately, the Search and Rescue Beacon (SARBE) functioned properly and provided a signal for the search-and-rescue teams of the RAF. One of the boats was almost 60 miles off course and it was lucky to be just within range of the Wessex helicopters. Again, I have to thank the helicopter crews for pulling our blokes out of the shit. Though we had been successful in liberating South Georgia without losing a man, none of us were under the illusion that things could not have been a lot worse. Without the skill and bravery of the Wessex pilots, we could be down maybe as many men as a troop. On top of that, we owed the Wasp crews for their crippling of the Argentinian submarine that could have been devastating to our force.

The *Santa Fe*'s crew were being detained by M Company, Royal Marines, along with the other Argentinian prisoners. I don't know the reasons why – possibly because he was trying to scuttle the sub – but one of the submariners was shot dead by one of the British guards. The submariner was buried with full military honours, and believe it or not, he was the only death, friendly or enemy, in the entire duration of Operation Paraquet and the retaking of South Georgia. That seemed almost remarkable given that by this point a submarine had been crippled at sea, two Wessex helicopters had crashed and three warships had fired from line astern – testament to the show of force that had convinced the enemy to surrender.

In many ways, South Georgia felt almost more like an exercise than a battle, especially for those of us who had watched from the sidelines, but we knew that the 155 prisoners we had taken were just a tiny part of the Argentinian force.

Waiting for us on the Falklands were another 10,000.

* * *

It was with sadness that I said goodbye to the stokers on the Red Plum and cross-decked to HMS *Brilliant*. After retaking South Georgia, it was decided that HMS *Endurance* would not be coming with us to the Falklands – as the famous saying goes, 'For you, the war is over'.

I often think of that vessel and her crew. She was a happy ship and served Britain proudly until 1991. The ship's motto, taken from the Shackleton family, was: 'By endurance we conquer'.

Words to live by!

There were 1,500km to cover before we got to the Falklands and so it's fair to say I had some time on my hands. We had Captain Astiz and his supply cupboard to keep an eye on, of course, but that duty came around rarely. Most of the time we would sit around and chat, sleep, do a bit of exercise and look out over the sea. I would also pen letters to Jenny. For this, we used a self-sealing piece of paper, the back of which formed the envelope. Named after the colour of the paper, these 'blueys' would be collected and taken by helicopter to either HMS *Leeds Castle* or HMS *Dumbarton Castle* – fast patrol ships that would shuttle mail back and forth to Ascension, where it would be flown home.

Given that we were almost the entirety of two hemispheres away, it was an incredibly efficient system and for good reason – if you want a man to fight well, keep his mind on what he needs to do. The less he has to worry about back home, the better. Of course, this could backfire, but in the climate of the Falklands War, I doubt there were many 'Dear John' letters in this campaign, such as I had received in Northern Ireland. This was a patriotic war and the country saw us as British heroes. To dump your husband or boyfriend at the time would not have gone down well with family and friends, I imagine. Not to say it didn't happen, but I never heard of such instances.

Jenny would write to me every day after she finished work at Bulmers Cider company. I didn't always receive her letters in order, but I always received a box of cigars just before each mission. Considering she had no idea what we were doing on operations, I always found this brilliant timing a little odd and it made me think back to my mum's story and how she had known my father was in trouble before she got the news that he'd been shot down. Perhaps it was all just coincidence and pure luck, but I'm open to the idea that we are all more connected than we realise.

As HMS *Brilliant*, HMS *Antrim* and HMS *Plymouth* made their way to join the rest of the British fleet gathering on the Falklands, we began to receive word on how diplomatic events surrounding the war were unfolding. The US Secretary of State, a retired general by the name of Alexander Haig, was President Ronald Reagan's envoy to meet and talk with both sides of the conflict. Reagan and British PM Margaret Thatcher seemed to be aligned politically and our divisions were side by side in Germany facing the Soviet threat. With this in mind, I'd assumed that America would express no favour to either side, but if they did, then it would be towards Britain.

Wrong!

It became clear that Haig favoured Argentina's claim over the islands and that felt like a massive kick in the teeth, not to mention a knife in the back!

I am writing this book in 2021, at the end of a 20-year war in which British soldiers fought and died in Afghanistan alongside our US allies. We did this because America was attacked on 9/11 and we answered the call to stand with her in war. We also fought beside them in Iraq in two wars, and of course, we were staunch allies in the fight against the Axis powers; the coalition headed by Nazi Germany, Japan, and fascist Italy.

For some reason, this sense of unity did not seem to exist in the seventies and eighties – at least not outside of the military. As it turned out, the Pentagon was doing all it could behind the scenes to help. Disaster for Britain would also mean disaster for NATO, the military alliance established by the North Atlantic Treaty of 1949 and so defence chiefs planned to loan Britain the USS Guam, an amphibious assault ship capable of carrying helicopters and Harriers, should we lose one of our carriers. They also aided with supplies – notable Sidewinder air-to-air missiles and fuel. That was behind closed doors, though.

In public, things were different. I imagine Northern Ireland almost certainly had something to do with it as a lot of Americans seemed to have a romantic notion that the IRA were just happy-go-lucky freedom fighters. I expect they would have thought differently had they seen what a pipe bomb does to women and children who had absolutely nothing to do with the past, or current, political situation. I'm glad that Britain and America have rediscovered their alliance in this century, but believe me when I tell you that it was just empty words during the Falklands. We went to war for America after 9/11. When the Falklands were invaded and British citizens were held hostage by a foreign power, the US Secretary of State's suggestion was that we should just roll over – thanks, pal! Thankfully, in Britain we had a prime minister with guts. As Thatcher once said during her 1981 Conservative Party Conference speech: 'The lady's not for turning.' And neither was the task force. With or without

America's diplomatic support, we would liberate the islands and our British people.

* * *

It was an incredible feeling to close in on the Falklands and see HMS *Hermes* and her attendant vessels soon after our mission to South Georgia. These frigates and destroyers, known as goalkeepers, were a last line of defence against an attack on the carrier. Should we lose our carriers, we would be without the ability to launch our own airpower and the losses to our own ships and men would be severe. Seeing Sidewinder-armed Sea Harriers take off from the deck of the *Hermes*, I felt a buzz of excitement knowing that we were drawing closer to the enemy. Over the horizon, dozens of other ships were gathering to close on the Falkland Islands.

This was it!

We boarded helicopters and cross-decked again from *Brilliant*, this time onto *Hermes*, our new home. At 236 metres long, she was a fair size bigger than the Red Plum!

The Task Force commander was on board this carrier, with the army's command working from HMS *Fearless*. Our regimental planning team was also on that amphibious assault vessel, headed by Colonel Mike Rose, a former Guards Division officer.

It was fascinating to be on board an aircraft carrier, not to mention noisy! I was once told that the decibel level of a

Harrier in takeoff is the same as a full stadium cheering when a goal is scored, so that gives you some idea of how hard it was to have a quiet chat with your mate! You could say that *Hermes* was a floating town as there were people on board who did every kind of job, from mechanic to cook to nurse to lawyer... yes, we even have those at sea, unfortunately. There's a lot of legality involved in wars, from rules of engagement to protecting the rights of service people, and so every time the British military goes to war, there are a few uniformed lawyers that go with it – there's no escaping them even on the battlefield, but more about that later.

Perhaps, with the regular departures of aircraft, 'hive' might be a better way to describe the busy vessel that never slept. There were Harriers and helicopters on the deck, with more in the cavernous hangars below. Though the Harriers were capable of vertical takeoff – a feat which had made them famous – there was also a ramp at the front of the carrier so that they could take off using less fuel and therefore have more time in the air.

In the Second World War it was the Spitfires and Hurricanes that would become famous for fighting the enemy's aircraft. In the Falklands, it would be the Harriers and in particular, the Sea Harrier. Armed with Sidewinder air-to-air missiles and a nose-mounted cannon, they were the guardian angels of the fleet and those who sailed within it. The RAF's Harrier GR3s had been developed for ground attack and reconnaissance, and they were armed with cannon, bombs and rocket pods. The pilots were masters of low-level flying and the purpose of these aircraft would be to soften enemy positions and provide close air support once the troops were ashore. Since the First World War aircraft had supported infantry operations; the infantry were now supported by ground attack aircraft and the infantry and ground attack aircraft were supported by fighters. The battlefields of the Falklands would stretch from trenches in the muddy earth to 40,000 feet in the sky.

I don't think there was ever any doubt that once ashore, the infantry of the British Army would defeat the enemy. We had brought with us the Royal Marines, the Paras (Parachute Regiment), the Guards and the Gurkhas. That is an infantry force that is the envy of any army in the world and many of the Argentinians that we would be fighting were conscripts who were there because they had to be and not through choice. Our soldiers had chosen this life and so they were ready.

Of course, it was one thing having this force and another getting them onto the islands. The *Santa Fe* had been knocked out, but there were other subs and there was still the threat of surface ships, most notably the cruiser *Belgrano*. All dangerous threats, but what worried us most was the Argentinian air power. Piloted by brave men, the aircraft ranged against us were as follows:

- 24 x Pucará ground attack aircraft

- 54 x A4 Skyhawks, split between Airforce and Naval assets
- 27 x Dagger
- 16 x Mirage
- 4 x Super Etendard

It was the Super Etendards that really worried us as these would carry the ship-destroying Exocet missiles. They had been supplied courtesy of our French 'allies', who had also provided Argentina with the Mirage multi-role fighters, meaning they could be employed both as fighters and ground attack aircraft. The Daggers were also multi-role jets and these had come from Israel. The A4 Skyhawks were produced in America and had been used to great effect by the US in Vietnam as a ground attack aircraft. The Pucará was also used in this role. A prop plane (meaning it has a propeller rather that a jet engine), it was the only enemy aircraft manufactured in Argentina and not by one of Britain's so-called allies!

Though our own aircraft were very good for the period, they were by no means streets ahead of the enemy's. This was peer against peer and losing air supremacy was a real possibility. If that was the case, our infantry would be hammered from the air by cannon fire, bombs, even napalm, a thick burning fuel that melts flesh from the bone. Knowing you have to fight an enemy in front of you, but worrying about attack from the air is a different thing altogether. For the most part an infantry soldier is powerless against it: you're the snake and they're the eagle swooping down with razor-sharp talons. We had been trained in a lot of things in the army – and air attack was to be a staple of any war with Russia – but none of us in D Squadron had experienced it before – I don't know if anyone in the fleet had either. The IRA and other insurgencies around the world had shot at us and bombed us, but it had been decades since the British Armed Forces had faced enemy planes.

The air war over the Falklands would be fierce, but at this point in the campaign, they were just a threat across the horizon and a thought in the back of our minds.

That would change soon enough.

* * *

Aboard the *Hermes* we put our precious stores and weapons alongside G Squadron's, and found ourselves, amid the hustle and bustle, a place where we could live. We assumed this living arrangement would be temporary as we were nearing the islands and G Squadron had already received their orders: they would act as the task force's forward reconnaissance element, deploying Observation Posts (OPs) and patrols to gather intelligence on the enemy. G Squadron's targets would include Port Stanley, Stanley Airfield, Goose Green, San Carlos, Ajax Bay, Darwin and Fitzroy Settlement on West Island. The Special Boat Service (SBS) would also be deploying teams, primarily to recce possible landing sites for the landing craft and ships.

Each recce patrol would have to survive for a month without resupply – everything that the men needed would have to be carried in with them, putting their equipment at well over 120lb each. Oh, how we smiled as we thought of the brigadier and his backwards jumper and his advice that no man should carry more than 40lb. *That's all well and good, sir, but what will we eat?*

As well as food, the men of G Squadron would need to carry picks, spades, hessian and chicken wire for building their hides. The terrain of the Falklands is soft peat and bog, so any digging would be into soaking-wet ground. Living in such conditions for a day is miserable, but G Squadron's men would have to do so for 30 days altogether. Some people wonder why such emphasis is placed on physical fitness in special forces selection, considering we spend a lot of our time 'in the job' in OPs, but the reason is simple: you need to be highly fit to stay functioning in adverse conditions. In other words, fit body, fit mind. If a man stops paying attention in an OP, even for a minute, he might miss vital information that could cost other people their lives.

To make their recces even more difficult there would be thick mists on the coastal targets. G Squadron patrol commanders would have to make decisions on whether they could observe from OPs, or if they'd have to lay up in the day and make close-target recces at night. This, of course, would bring with it the danger of being spotted by the enemy, or worse: walking into minefields. The enemy had been sewing them in front of their positions and there was little chance of finding them except with your feet. There were night vision devices available to us in the sabre squadrons, but they were in the early days of the technology and not much use without a clear sky and starlight.

The rations that the lads would be carrying in were known as a 'rat pack' – a combination of biscuits and tins that could give you one good 'scoff' a day if you combined a few items together. It was heavier than the later rat packs, which had boil-in-the-bag meals rather than tins. There were also 10-man ration packs which had larger tins and a wider variety of menus than the individual packs. These were definitely prized items to scrounge – when you're miserable and lying in a wet and cold OP for days, a little variety in your diet can make your day!

Despite what they'd be eating and the conditions on the ground, G Squadron were looking forward to getting onto the Falklands – there's always pride in being the first, not to mention the opportunity to be closest to the enemy. After the success of South Georgia, the regiment was full of confidence, but the war would soon give us a reality check we would never forget.

* * *

The beginning of May 1982 was a mixed bag for the task force.

On the 1st, a Vulcan bomber from the RAF took off from Ascension Island and headed south. After air-to-air refuelling with several VC10s over the South Atlantic – 15 times! – the Vulcan surprised the Argentinian forces on the Falkland Islands and attempted to bomb the runway at Port Stanley.

The bombing itself proved to be ineffectual, but you had to take your hat off to the Vulcan and the tanker crews. As far as endurance goes it was an incredible feat and included a period of flying the Vulcan at 91 metres above sea level to avoid enemy radar. Despite the bombs doing little physical damage, this was Britain's first offensive action on the islands and told the enemy 'we can reach you, and we're coming'. For young conscript soldiers, I imagine the site of the big bomber scared the shit out of them. Who knows how that fear would factor in over the coming weeks, but I have to think it played a part in convincing many of them to surrender. The drip, drip, drip of seeing enemy men and materials can break even a determined man. As we would later see in the Gulf, bombing is as much about psychology as it is about physical damage.

I was meant to be attending a wedding on the day of the first Vulcan raid. I was best man to a good friend who had failed selection and then left the army. Before you start to feel sorry for him, he set up a business when he got out and is now a multimillionaire – funny where our paths lead us in life! Back down in the South Atlantic, the task force command decided that the Harriers might have more luck than the Vulcans and followed up the Vulcan by sending 12 Harriers towards Port Stanley.

This wasn't something that I wanted to miss. As the aircraft lined up on deck and prepared for takeoff, a few of us decided to sneak closer for a look. We ended up on a walkway beneath the deck at the aircraft turnaround point and the heat and noise above us was hypnotising, although that might have been the effect of breathing in so much jet fuel!

The 12 harriers launched and attacked the airfield with bombs and cannon fire. The Argentinians responded with anti-aircraft fire and missiles. We didn't see any of the action as it was all well over the horizon from us, but we held our breath for news.

As the BBC correspondent Brian Hanrahan reported: 'We counted them all out and we counted them all back in.'

The Harriers came back with no losses! The Argentinians claimed to have downed two of them, but their gunners must have been huffing aviation gas themselves because all 12 of the aircraft made it back to the ship. Most were in one piece, except for one Harrier that had a hole punched through its tailfin – a lucky escape. Much like the Vulcan raid, the damage caused by the Harriers was not significant, but it left the Argentinians with the knowledge that we meant business. If they wanted the Falkland Islands, they would have to pay for them.

Alas, it is always young men who pay the price of their commanders' stubbornness and grand delusions, and we saw the truth of this the next day.

On 2 May, the Argentine light cruiser *Belgrano* was steaming towards the Falkland Islands. I think it's fair to say that she wasn't coming towards the task force for any other reason than sinking our ships and killing our men. Unfortunately for the crew of the *Belgrano* – a vessel bought from America – HMS *Conqueror* saw them before they saw us. *Conqueror* was a nuclear submarine and as the *Belgrano* was within the 200-mile exclusion zone that Britain had placed around the islands, the sub fired two torpedoes, hitting the *Belgrano* below the waterline.

The damage done to the ship was massive, as was the loss of life. Over 300 souls died that day and I imagine many of them in the most terrible of circumstances. That is not something to be cheered for, but nor is it something to be misunderstood. Make no mistake, the crew of the *Belgrano* were coming to kill us but *Conqueror* killed them first. What happened was ugly and tragic, but that is exactly what war is. Indeed, even the *Belgrano*'s captain would later say should he have encountered a British vessel, then he would have done the same thing and engaged with the intent to destroy. There is only one way to avoid loss of life in wars and that is not to have them in the first place!

Ships from Argentina and Chile later rescued more than 700 men, but they were delayed by fog and bad weather. It must have been a terrible ordeal for the stricken crew, and while I have sympathy, I have none for the ridiculous arguments that the *Conqueror* should not have fired, which is something that has been said by armchair admirals and politicians in the years that followed. If you don't want to lose your ship, don't invade another country's territory – it's quite simple. Besides, as events proved a few days later, the Argentinians clearly had no compunction about sinking our own vessels.

On 4 May, HMS *Sheffield*, *Coventry* and *Glasgow* were operating as part of the fleet's anti-aircraft picket. In many ways, the role was similar to that performed by the skirmishers of the Rifle Brigade, except these ships were not in place to deter infantry, but Argentinian jets, the most dangerous being the Super Etendard and the Exocet missile that it carried.

Sheffield was the southernmost of the three destroyers. As well as a threat from enemy aircraft, there was also a danger of submarines and so the captain of the ship had ordered course changes every 90 seconds to avoid giving the subs an easy target. Unbeknown to them, that day, two Argentinian pilots were flying at 30 metres above the waves to close on the ships and avoid the British radar. This was a technique perfected by practising against their own vessels, which were the same type as the *Sheffield* – one had been built in Cumbria!

It wasn't until the Etendards popped up to get their own radar fix on the British ships that they came to the attention of HMS *Glasgow*, which immediately went to action stations and initiated 'handbrake' – the process of turning into an attack to provide a smaller target, while firing chaff and flares to throw off a missile's guidance. *Glasgow*'s crew stood by its defensive weaponry and sent a warning to *Sheffield*, but this was not received due to an unauthorised use of the *Sheffield*'s satellite communication system. A few seconds later, the Exocet was launched towards an unsuspecting vessel.

The first the crew of the *Sheffield* knew of the attack was when lookouts spotted smoke from the missile. Despite this potential sign of enemy attack, the bridge officers did not call the captain to the bridge, nor go to action stations – meaning systems like the Sea Dart missile would not be armed and in position to engage the Exocet.

Two Exocets had been fired at the *Sheffield*. The first was spotted splashing into the sea a half mile away.

The second slammed into her starboard side.

It's not for me to tell you what went on aboard that ship. I can only say that it must have been terrifying. Truth be told, confusion reigned throughout the fleet until a Lynx helicopter landed on the *Hermes*, carrying a couple of the *Sheffield*'s officers, who confirmed the strike on their ship.

Escort ships had been dispatched by the fleet to investigate and now Sea King helicopters began to ferry the survivors onto *Hermes*. *Sheffield*'s fire-fighting system had been taken out by the missile and though afloat, the ship was ablaze and was being abandoned.

With the other medics in the squadron I ran up to the deck to help with the wounded. They were in a mess, understandably shocked and many of them suffering horrific burns, including those whose synthetic uniforms had melted onto their flesh. It was my first time seeing casualties at the hands of the enemy and I was more determined than ever to get to grips with them.

An aircraft carrier is a noisy place at the best of times, but now this was accompanied by the moans of the wounded and the shouts of the confused. Some survivors were asking after friends, others staring out into space. Of the 281 crew on board, 20 were killed in the attack. The survivors were transferred to an RFA vessel and taken back to Ascension. It must have been a terrible way to end a war – struck by an unseen foe and never getting the chance to retaliate.

It's funny how an infantryman in Northern Ireland would be fined a month's pay for losing a single bullet, but the senior crew could lose their ship without sanction. To not go to action stations once the lookouts spotted smoke is unforgivable – if it turns out to be a false alarm, so what? You're in a war zone, you know the enemy is out there. What better things do you have to do than go to action stations?

Only one body of the 20 souls lost was ever recovered. As for HMS *Sheffield*, she foundered while being towed to Ascension and now rests in the ocean as a Commonwealth war memorial.

The 4th of May was a dark day for the task force, and it was not the last.

* * *

After the loss of the *Sheffield* we were all a little more on edge about the Argentine air threat and looking forward to getting our boots onto terra firma. Of course, we also wanted to hit back against the enemy – revenge is a powerful motivator.

Our squadron commander, Cedric Delves, had begun referring to us as 'buccaneers' because we were bouncing around ships between missions, not to mention wearing an odd assortment of DPM (disruptive pattern material, rather than the plain khaki uniforms of old) and civilian clothing, and he was working hard to find us a target that would allow us to follow up the success of South Georgia. Most of the obvious targets were on the main island, still some distance away, but then we caught a lucky break: air photography from a Harrier showed positive proof that there were enemy aircraft on Pebble Island, close to West Falkland. Confirmatory recce flights identified most of these planes as Pucará ground attack aircraft – in other words, the aircraft they'd use to attack our landing forces and kill our lads.

It didn't take Cedric long to draw up his plan – a textbook raid against an enemy airfield. I don't think I'd ever been more excited in my life. This was vintage SAS work, as pioneered by David Stirling against Rommel and the Afrika Korps. This was everything that the regiment was made for and everything I'd dreamed of – *Sergeant Rock, eat your heart out!*

Our OC took the plan to the task force commander and…

He rejected it out of hand.

We were gutted. Furious. Why were we even there if we weren't going to be allowed to do our jobs? Having seen the survivors of the *Sheffield*, we wanted to avenge them. We wanted to hit back.

With hindsight, I can see that the task force command was probably just too busy with the fallout of the Exocet attack to dedicate the time to look into, sign off on and plan a raid. It's understandable, but we felt like attacks similar to what happened to the *Sheffield* would continue unless we could impact the enemy's air power. Our OC understood this, as did the regiment's CO. Shortly after the two got together on the *Fearless*, Colonel Rose suggested that intelligence pointed to a radar site on Pebble Island. As the island stood close to the approach to San Carlos – the intended landing site for the amphibious operation – any radar would easily detect the approach of the vessels and so needed to be neutralised.

The OC met with the task force command again. This second time, the navy latched onto the idea immediately. Cedric Delves and D Squadron would be given four days to plan and execute the raid, and Admiral Woodward told the OC that he wasn't interested in destroying the enemy aircraft:

'I want that radar site,' he said.

We were in business.

*　*　*

Before we could carry out a raid we needed a recce and with only four days to plan and execute, we needed it quickly.

Boat Troop were the obvious choice. The plan was to insert them onto West Falkland at Purvis Point. Then, using Clipper canoes, which are just like what civilians use for recreation out on the lakes, they would cross the inlet between the islands. Two men would be left as security for the canoes, while the other six would disperse at various points along Pebble Island to provide a radio relay to the heavier, more powerful radios held within the canoes.

The heli insertion went well, but the row across the inlet was understandably arduous work, the troopers fighting against strong currents, lashing rain and choppy waters. The eight men were freezing and exhausted by the time they arrived on Pebble Island, but there was still work to be done and they did it well, relaying vital information back about the airfield and settlement, including positions of the enemy aircraft.

As the intelligence picture built, the OC planned his attack: Boat Troop would act as the guides for the rest of the mission, leading us to our start line and confirming we were orientated correctly to our targets. Mobility Troop would be the attack force, Air Troop would provide first support and Mountain Troop would be in reserve. I felt gutted for the Mountain Troop lads, whose only real chance of getting into the action was if things went wrong.

A tough break!

On the night of the raid, 14 May, I prepared my weapon and equipment for the fight ahead. I stripped my magazines, tested the springs and clicked in one round after another. After checking my grenades, both smoke and high-explosive, I fitted them snugly in my gear. I stripped and cleaned my weapon, ensuring the working parts were lubricated so that they would feed and eject the rounds without stoppages. Then I checked over my medical kit, ensuring that I had anything needed to deal with severe battlefield casualties. The minor ones could wait until we got back to the ship, but if a major bleed isn't treated instantly, then a casualty can die in minutes. I wasn't worried about my own safety – that's not bravado, just the truth – but I couldn't live with the thought that I could lose a teammate because I hadn't prepared enough. Some things in battle you can't control, others you can, and I wasn't about to go into action half-cocked.

Constantly altering course to try and shake off the threat of submarines, HMS *Hermes* closed on Pebble Island. The weather was atrocious, freezing rain driving across in sheets. It was miserable to be in, but that makes for good weather for special forces: the enemy would be more concerned about keeping dry than keeping guard.

The OC came close to calling the attack off – I expect because he was worried about flying conditions rather than his men getting wet – but the pilots were up to the job and with straining engines, the four Sea King helis lifted up from the deck of HMS *Hermes* and took off towards the enemy. They carried the entirety of D Squadron, more than 50 special forces soldiers raring to get at the enemy.

Sitting in the back, we were all smiles. We'd packed as much ammunition as we could and planned on using it. When war broke out, I'd thought that the politicians would sort something out before a shot was fired – now, those days were long gone. The *Belgrano* was at the bottom of the ocean, as was the *Sheffield*. South Georgia had almost felt more like a training exercise rather than a war, but we were under no illusion what we were about to do tonight – we were flying to Pebble Island to kill the enemy.

I didn't have any compunction about that. It's not that I was a bloodthirsty maniac who wanted to kill for the sake of killing – if I was, I could have shot the assassin that I had dead to rights in Northern Ireland but I hadn't needed to pull the trigger then and so I hadn't. This raid would be different. As fire support, we would be laying down the suppressing fire that would allow Mobility Troop to get close to the airfield and attack. If we didn't do our jobs properly, our comrades in Mobility would pay the price. There was no thought of hesitation or failure – we hadn't come this far to be anything but the best.

It was a rough ride in the Sea Kings and the rain lashed at us as we disembarked at Purvis Cove. We were met by the troop commander and Boat Troop guides, Cedric Delves having flown ahead, and the boss gave us our confirmatory orders. He seemed calm and on the level. We were all excited, but we controlled it and acted with professionalism.

We shouldered our kit – a full battle load along with 2 x 81mm mortar rounds apiece. It was like having another man on your back and we were about to cover seven kilometres across uneven and boggy ground – there's a reason why selection starts on the hills!

We set off in double file, but due to the terrain we soon switched into single and a line of soldiers began to snake its way towards the enemy. Due to the weather and flying conditions we were a little behind schedule and then became further delayed when one of Mobility Troop managed to wander off the track and get lost – muppet! Two of the group went to look for him as the rest of us pressed on through the night.

Despite the weight on my back, it was an enjoyable tab for me as I thought of what lay in store. I had lived a good life, I had been raised by good parents and I was loved by my wife, but I knew without doubt that this was the moment my life had been leading up to.

There was no place in the world I would rather be.

Reaching the RV (rendezvous), we dropped our 81mm rounds off where the mortar team were digging in the tube and baseplate. With boggy ground, it was imperative that it was solidly mounted or rounds could go off course with tragic consequences.

With Mobility Troop delayed by their missing man, Mountain Troop were ordered to switch from reserve to assault force and my mate John's smile was one of pure delight: 'Let slip the dogs of war!'

Our own troop started to move forwards. At first, our plan had been to move to a structure known as the woolshed and from there, we would go into the settlement to establish communications with the locals. However, with the intelligence that the Argentinian Marines had mixed themselves in with the local populace, we decided there was too much at risk and so the plan to advance on the woolshed was dropped. A good thing, as it turns out, as we later discovered that there were 200 of the enemy dug in and around it. Instead, we would cause a distraction by laying down fire to the woolshed's flanks and into areas where the rounds would not risk hitting civilians.

The battle was initiated with a 'woomp' as the 81mm mortar opened fire – it was the first and only round that it would fire as the baseplate sank deeply into the bog and had to be dug out! At about the same time, Mobility Troop finally arrived at the RV, only to find out they were now in reserve – I can only imagine the look on their faces!

Naval gunfire from HMS *Glamorgan* began to slam into the enemy positions on Big Mountain, which overlooked the settlement and airfield. The vessel also fired illumination rounds into the sky, bathing the airfield and its surroundings in an eerie yellow glow designed to help our assault.

Mountain Troop wasted no time and began destroying the aircraft with explosive chargers, 40mm rounds from their underslung grenade launchers and small arms fire – they even went so far as to rip the instruments out of some of the aircraft by hand.

Over in Air Troop, we opened fire to the flanks of the woolshed and only got some sporadic fire in return. It was my first time ever shooting at an enemy and I was a little disappointed at the lack of resistance. Their Marines were definitely not cut from the same cloth as our Bootnecks and the enemy seemed quite happy to cower and wait for us to destroy their aircraft and go away. So far in the campaign, the only 'cojones' displayed from the enemy had come from their pilots. Their infantry didn't even want to get in on the fight on Pebble Island, it seemed, despite them outnumbering us three to one at the very least. Our surprise attack had knocked them out of the fight before they were ever in it, such is the psychological damage of a special forces raid.

Perhaps feeling left out of the battle himself, our troop sergeant ordered us across the open ground in front of the woolshed. If the enemy had his act together this would have been dangerous, but we got across the killing ground without incident. Evidently, however, the sergeant didn't like this new spot – no sooner had we got there than he ordered us back to our first position! We did as we were instructed, only to be told to cross back again. I couldn't believe what was happening. In the light of the illumination rounds we looked at each other in disbelief, then came the order to move *yet again*, crossing the open ground for the fourth time – were we conducting a raid, or a bleep test?

One of our corporals decided it was time to have a quiet word with the sergeant and rugby-tackled him to the floor and started hitting him. A few of the lads pulled them off each other and our shuttle runs came to an end. We put down more fire to the flanks of the woolshed, but it became pretty clear that we weren't going to face stiff resistance as enemy aircraft after enemy aircraft went up in flames. Soon, every single one of them on the airfield was destroyed.

The officer commanding gave the order to cease fire. The small arms died away, but then came the sound of an explosion. Two of Mountain Troop were caught up in the blast of what we reckoned must have been a command detonated charge. Fortunately, neither of the men's injuries were life-threatening and they were helped back to the squadron rendezvous, which was different to our insertion point. That had been at far more of a distance so that we could sneak in undetected. Now that things had kicked off, the time for stealth was behind us.

Air Troop collapsed back towards it as well. I was still buzzing with adrenaline and the 700-metre tab passed in no time. The Sea Kings started to come in and collect the troops, with Air Troop providing security. We would be the last troop taken out and, inspired by Colonel Hal Moore at the Battle of the Ia Drang Valley (later immortalised by Mel Gibson in the movie, *We Were Soldiers*), I wanted to be the last one to leave the island and the battlefield. I waited until the rest of the troop were on board before climbing through the Sea King's door, looking back out of it as we took off.

Climbing over the black sea and gaining altitude, I looked down and saw the brightly burning pyres that had shortly before been enemy aircraft. The feeling of elation was almost overwhelming. I wondered if this was how the original SAS troopers had felt after their raids in North Africa, almost exactly 40 years earlier, and the words engraved into the clock tower at Hereford came into my mind:

We are the Pilgrims, master; we shall go
Always a little further...

9
PILGRIMS

D Squadron were victorious and riding high on victory.

To say that the raid on Pebble Island was a success would be a massive understatement. In a little under 30 minutes, Mountain Troop had destroyed 11 enemy aircraft – a massive blow to the Argentinians' capability to contest the landings and to support their infantry once ours was on the ground. Furthermore, it was a great blow to their morale. We had come in the night, killed, destroyed and withdrawn, leaving behind nothing but empty shell cases and the burning wreckage of their planes. If that doesn't put the shits up a soldier, I don't know what will – the professionals had arrived on the battlefield!

Not only had D Squadron destroyed the enemy aircraft, but the fuel dump had also been taken out. There was no sign of the radar site, but after the success of destroying the aircraft, I don't think anyone cared.

When we landed on the *Hermes*, a scene like that at the end of the *Top Gun* movie ensued – albeit one under grey rainy skies and without a pair of Ray-Bans in sight! The SAS troopers were shaking hands and celebrating with the crews of the helis and the *Hermes*.

In the midst of the celebrations, suddenly a shot rang out. We knew it couldn't have been an enemy shot and looked around for the culprit: Scobie had accidentally discharged his weapon into the deck and narrowly missed hitting a member of Mountain Troop who lay concussed in the sick bay! With mates like that, who needs enemies?!

We were elated at the success of the raid. I imagine that must be how it feels to win at the Olympics, only our stakes had been life and death, rather than a position on a podium. D Squadron and the regiment had two major successes under its belt in a month and we had done so with only a couple of light casualties. We were on cloud nine and felt invincible.

A few days later, though, everything changed.

* * *

We had routed the enemy without loss on South Georgia and taken 11 of his aircraft out of the game on Pebble Island. The US Navy SEALs have a saying, 'the only easy day was yesterday', and it's a good one to live by, but all was looking well in D Squadron's world as we were riding high on the tide of victory.

The first news that cut back our feeling of invincibility was a 'blue on blue' – the term given to the friendly fire incidents that plague military campaigns. War is a confusing business. The nature of intelligence gathering is that you are going into the unknown and this can lead to fatal accidents. Sometimes they are caused by the terrain, other times by the weapons and men of your own side.

G Squadron had remained undetected in their hides on the Falkland Islands. Unfortunately, a patrol from the Special Boat Service was operating in the wrong location. Mistaking each other for the enemy, a firefight broke out and the patrol commander from the SBS was killed. It was a costly blow and a tragedy felt by all of the task force's special forces troops.

G Squadron's mission was not in vain, however, and they were passing vital information back to the planning staff. We didn't hear any of it ourselves, except to be told that G were doing themselves proud. We'd find out in time, surely enough, as the next stage in the campaign could only be the landings on the islands. After the death of the SBS officer, we were all eager to get onto a mission and focus on that, but tragedy was not done with us.

In D Squadron, we were chuffed to bits with the news that we would be the Direct Action (DA) unit for the foreseeable future and quite possibly the entirety of the war. To sum up the job in a nutshell, it would fall on us to conduct the raids on the enemy. As far as special forces roles went, I felt like we'd won the lottery.

All of D and part of G Squadrons were aboard the carrier HMS *Hermes*. I wonder how the lads of G Squadron felt, having spent weeks lying in the mud, while we in D Squadron had been lucky enough to conduct a raid that would live on in regimental lore? Personally, I'd have been pretty gutted, but that's just how it goes in the military. By now I'd seen enough to know that what goes around comes around and I was going to ride our wave of good fortune for as long as it lasted. Sometimes you get to be the one doing the mission that everyone's talking about, sometimes you're watching it on the TV with everyone else – not even John Rambo can be everywhere.

Four days after we had successfully returned from Pebble Island, the time came for us buccaneers to move to a new home yet again and this time we cross-decked from *Hermes* to *Intrepid* – one of the two amphibious assault ships in the fleet. It was no easy thing to move all of our troops and gear, but as usual, 846 Sea King Squadron were up to the task. They were to become the workhorse of the campaign, flying thousands of hours in adverse weather and with the ever-present threat of enemy fighters and anti-aircraft fire. It was 846 who had transported us to and from Pebble Island. Without them, the SAS would never have been able to conduct the raid. They deserve as much credit as anyone.

We had a lot of gear to move into our new home. One of G Squadron's SNCOs (senior non-commissioned officers) – Paddy – had joined us and brought 'gifts' courtesy of America's Delta Force, which I will talk more about in a moment.

Delta are modelled on the SAS and the operators in both have an excellent working relationship and mutual respect.

I went on to spend some great times in their home of Fort Bragg in the late eighties and early nineties and was honoured to carry the foundation stone – the first ceremonial stone to be laid for a new building – for their barracks at Hereford. They even entrusted me with a Chinook once, loaning me the heli to fly from Bragg to collect the incoming troop from Raleigh – only in America do you get that kind of service.

I was lucky enough to speak with the founder of Delta, Colonel Charlie Beckwith, on several occasions in my career. He and his second-in-command, Bucky Burrows, were both veterans of the war in Vietnam (1955–75) and true soldiers' soldiers. Charlie wrote a book, *Delta Force*,* which I recommend. Both men fought an uphill battle to establish Delta, but thanks to them, America has one of the world's greatest special forces units.

Because Paddy was catching up with the task force, the 'gifts' from Delta did not come to the Falklands via ship. Paddy was flown over the Atlantic in a C130, then parachuted into the ocean with weapons from America. The canisters containing the gifts – and Paddy! – were then collected by the navy.

The best part of the unexpected surprise was Stinger air-to-ground missiles, which the Mujahideen of Afghanistan would soon use against the Soviet Union. A fire-and-forget weapon, they weighed a third of Britain's equivalent system:

---

* *Delta Force*, Charlie Beckwith, 1983.

the blow-pipe. The only downside was that their operation was a little complicated, as we would soon discover. There were also M209 rocket launchers, which are multiple buried, box-shaped weapons that fire 4x incendiary rounds. They were bulky bits of kit, but that didn't stop one of our lads humping one around for the rest of the campaign – I'm pretty sure that he never fired it!

Usually, moving weapons and materials from one ship to another was done with health and safety in mind, but time and helicopters were both in short supply, the enemy was near and so necessity trumped safety. Life jackets and seating were abandoned. Instead, we piled the back of the aircraft full of kit, then clambered in on top of it, ready to be carried from the *Hermes* to the *Intrepid*.

It was a long day, with kit loaded on one deck, followed by a short flight and then unloading on the other deck. Even in the cold air, it was warm work and thankfully, the rain wasn't lashing down for a change.

Myself and Air Troop had been flown from *Hermes* to the *Intrepid* just before day turned to night and the work of unloading and sorting kit continued into the dark hours. After piling our gear up on *Intrepid*'s flight deck, we watched as the Sea King flew across back to *Hermes* to collect what would be the final lift. This last flight would made up of G and D Squadron HQs, Mountain Troop and a two-man forward air controller team from the RAF. I was looking forward to them joining us on the *Intrepid* so that we could unload the last of the kit and get it housed on the new vessel. Once that was done, we'd be able to get a hot scoff inside us and find a place to bed down.

With a few of the other lads, I stood in the cold and watched and waited for the last flight to arrive. I watched as it took off from the deck, the aircraft's navigation light blinking as it rose into the air. I tracked it as it came across the water towards us, a helicopter full of my friends and comrades.

The Sea King's navigation light blinked: on, off, on, off, on, off…

The light had disappeared.

We looked at each other.

I felt a knot grow in my stomach as I looked back out to sea.

The light did not come back.

I started to feel sick. I told myself that maybe the light had failed, but I *knew*. Deep down, I knew something awful had happened.

Moments later, someone shouted the confirmation: 'The Sea King's down!'

The deck of the *Intrepid* became a sea of commotion: the heli had ditched, our blokes were in the water. That was dangerous at the best of times, but at night, with a cabin full of gear and men…

We started to wonder: had the final flight done what we had done to save space in the back of the heli, and ditched their life jackets?

Search lights began to criss-cross the choppy waters. Boats went out. I'd never felt as useless as I did in those moments. There was nothing that any of us from the squadron could do except wait for news from the search-and-rescue crews. Those were our mates and comrades that they were looking for and while we didn't want to give up hope, we were realists: there was little hope that everyone was coming out of the black waters alive.

Knowing that would be the case didn't make it any easier when we were given the confirmation. Nine men were pulled out of the sea alive. Twenty-two others died, including 20 from the regiment. Many of them were entombed in the Sea King that sank into the ocean's depths. The violence of the crash would have killed some on impact and knocked others unconscious. We could only hope that they had been spared the agony of drowning, or the terror of knowing that they could not escape.

Two men were recovered back to the *Intrepid*. One was Dave Hulme, the squadron medic. The other was a crewman from the helicopter. He was dead on arrival. An army chaplain came over and asked that I take the crewman's hand while he delivered the Last Rites.

It was cold and lifeless, and this moment spooked me more than any other during the campaign. Not so long ago, this man had been doing the job that he'd signed up for, with the rest of his life ahead of him. A split second changed all of that: he would not be going home, he had made the ultimate sacrifice.

The chaplain finished giving the Last Rites and so I placed his hand back on the stretcher. It was a picture that would be etched in my mind for the rest of my life. After saying my own silent and simple prayer for the departed crewman, I went back over to my troop to await more news.

Dave Hulme was suffering from hypothermia and was placed in a hot bath below decks. We later found out that he'd been the last man out of the helicopter and thankfully, he made a full recovery. Another survivor, 'Splash' Aston, would later write an account of the tragedy: *SAS: Sea King Down.**

I've been asked if Splash's nickname was related to the crash as military men often use gallows humour. But it was not, as I knew him when we were on selection together and he was called it back then. It turned out to be just one of life's dark coincidences. He and the other survivors had been through a terrible ordeal and were repatriated to the UK, but they were not done with their service. Splash continued his long career within the army, which had included two Wessex crashes on the glacier. He and some of the other Mountain Troop survivors had been involved in three helicopter crashes in less than a month – I don't know if that makes him incredibly lucky, or awfully unlucky.

---

* *SAS: Sea King Down*, by Mark Aston and Stuart Tootal, 2021.

Those of us who hadn't been involved in the crash were shell-shocked to say the least. The number of losses was equivalent to half a squadron and was the biggest loss of life in the regiment since the Second World War. I found it especially hard to accept the death of Paul Bunker, a close friend of mine. It was a sad end for a great soldier. We also lost Squadron Sergeant Majors Lawrence Gallagher (D Squadron) and Mick Atkinson (G Squadron) and Mountain Troop Sergeant Phil Curass (D Squadron). Also on board was Bill Begley (G Squadron) a small, humorous Irishman who had done selection with me. We were fairly close, Bill and I. In addition, on board and lost were a number of SNCOs with experience that would be much needed in the days to come. Corporal Wally Walpole (2 RGJ) served in the same infantry battalion as me and came to Hereford to serve in the squadron's stores.

All were great men and a hard act to follow.

They are deeply missed.

Not long after the incident, and while many of us were still numb from the tragedy, the officer commanding came on board to brief what remained of G and D Squadrons. I remember very little of what he said, but a line from one officer will stick in my mind forever: 'The regiment needs to be seen to be taking casualties,' he said.

I couldn't believe what I'd just heard and assumed I must be mistaken, but looking to the faces left and right of me, I wasn't the only one who was insulted and shocked by what he'd just heard. *Seen to be taking casualties?* We'd just lost 22 of our mates and comrades and another nine were being repatriated to the UK to recover from hypothermia and exposure. G and D Squadrons were down about 25 per cent of our strength – how many more casualties would the officer like?

At the time I was furious with the person who spoke those words, but now, as I write this, I am convinced that he was just repeating something that the brigadier had passed down to him from a cushy office in the UK – probably while wearing his jumper back to front. It just doesn't fit with the character of our officer that he'd say something like that without having the words put in his mouth. At least, I really hope that is the case.

The Sea King crash really brought home to me how quickly things can change in life, let alone war. One minute, Mountain Troop had been riding high on the back of a massive success, one that would live on forever in regimental lore. A few days later, they were fighting for their lives in the cold black waters. It was a sobering thought to say the least. Once it was obvious that it would be a shooting war, I'd expected that we'd lose a couple of men to the enemy, but to lose that many – and in an accident! – was an even more bitter pill to swallow. A dead albatross had been found at the scene where the Sea King ditched and while no one knew how it happened, bird strike (where a bird goes into a propeller and causes it to fail) or pilot error due to fatigue were the most likely causes of the crash.

Back in the UK, reports were breaking about the incident, but the news was reporting that it was Royal Marines on board.

The next of kin of the nine survivors were called into camp to be told that their loved ones were on the way home. The regimental families officer also went house to house to inform the widows that the worst had happened. Certainly, being the one to deliver that news is one of the hardest roles in any war. And receiving it? I can't even begin to imagine what those families went through.

Hereford is a small town and the regiment is smaller still. Word of the crash spread quickly and it reached Jenny. My wife rushed to camp to find out if anything had happened to me, but she was assured that I was OK. The following morning, she actually woke with a shock of grey hair in her golden curls! This would happen to her again in 1991 when I was out in the Gulf. Sometimes it's a lot easier to be the one on the front line: you know when you're in danger and when you're not, and although luck is involved in war, you do feel like there's things you can control. For the loved ones at home, all they have is uncertainty.

The crash was a real wake-up moment for me. I still believed I would be going home, but now I knew that I needed to be on top of my game at all times to make that happen. Cloudy minds would get us killed and so we pushed our feelings deep down inside of us. There was no such thing as a counsellor in those days. The memories and emotions would come once we were home. There was not even time for a service for our fallen brothers.

We had a war to fight.

10

RETAKE THE ISLANDS

The Argentinian forces were entrenched on the Falkland Islands. The Royal Navy and Royal Fleet Auxiliary had carried the troops from Great Britain but that meant nothing unless the infantry could be landed so that they could close with, and destroy, the enemy. Putting troops ashore is a difficult proposition – anyone who has seen the film *Saving Private Ryan* will understand why – and though the coastline of the Falklands was not defended like Hitler's Atlantic Wall, a series of formidable defences built on the French coast, it would still be an incredibly vulnerable moment for the troops. There's nowhere to hide on the water and one direct hit on a landing craft from an artillery shell could cost dozens and dozens of lives. The fleet had helicopters, but there were thousands of men to get ashore, not to mention all of their arms and ammunition.

A landing from sea was essential for victory.

San Carlos Water was the place chosen for this endeavour and under cover of darkness on the night of 21 May, British vessels began taking up position in the bay. When the Argentinians finally became aware of what had transpired, they retaliated with fury. I don't think anyone expected that the task force would come through this phase of the operation without casualties and sadly, that soon proved to be true.

Although we had destroyed 11 enemy aircraft on the Pebble Island raid, more Pucarás were flown in to replace them. The Argentinians knew their best – and in my opinion, their *only* – chance of winning the war was from the air and the enemy responded to the vessels in San Carlos with wave upon wave of air raids. During these times, the air would be loud with the sound of roaring jet engines and all kinds of fire from the British weapons that aimed to bring them down. From missiles to machine guns, everything but the kitchen sink was thrown skywards. You had to admire the bravery of their pilots, flying into such a storm of anti-aircraft fire at extremely low altitudes. The enemy lost a total of 13 aircraft across the islands that day, but also drew blood of their own.

Over the next few days, both HMS *Ardent* and HMS *Antelope* were hit by bombs dropped from Skyhawks and eventually sank. At sea, HMS *Coventry* was struck by bombs and the SS *Atlantic Conveyor* was struck and sunk by an Exocet missile. Nineteen men were killed aboard the Coventry, 12 on the *Atlantic Conveyor*.

Five Chinook helicopters also went down with the *Atlantic Conveyor*. These workhorses had been a key part of the plan for moving the infantry and supplies across the islands, and losing them meant that the bulk of the infantry would have to tab across the island – no enviable task in the lashing rain and cold of the South Atlantic. Incredibly, *Bravo November* – the one Chinook airframe rescued from the *Conveyor* – not only served in the Falklands conflict, but also went on to take part in operations in Iraq and Afghanistan.

Now there was a helicopter that was as keen as I was!

Of course, we knew very little of all this activity at the time. As direct action squadron, targets for raids were being identified by HQ and as troopers, we were gearing up for our missions.

It was time to retake the islands.

*   *   *

My path to the Falkland Islands was typical of many British soldiers. I had been through basic training honed and developed from centuries of near-constant warfare by Britain and her empire. Those who had trained me had fought in insurgencies around the world and those who had trained them had fought in Korea. The people who had trained them had fought in the Second World War. Those who had trained them had fought in the First World War. The people who had trained them had fought in the Boer War. And so it went on, war after war, lesson after lesson bought and paid for with blood and distilled into the training of a British Army soldier.

And that was just our basic and infantry training. Then there was Junior and Senior Brecon, which forges the finest infantry NCOs in the world. And beyond that, as an SAS trooper, I had received the best training that a soldier could receive. There were no finer soldiers on the planet and if there were any units that could say that they matched us as peers, they were certainly not part of the Argentinian military.

Compare their training to ours. Many of their 'Commandos' were given a four-week crash course following conscription at the beginning of the year.

Four weeks.

A British infantry soldier's *basic* training was three times as long as their 'Commando' training. Our own Royal Marine Commandos had received *32 weeks*, not to mention the continuation training carried out at every regiment. Every single British soldier sent to the Falklands had spent more time on a single exercise than the Argentinian conscripts had been given to go to war.

Only a fool wants to go to war at a disadvantage, but still, you could feel sorry for the Argie conscripts – imagine being 18 years old, given a month of training and then told to wait on a mountain for the world's best-trained soldiers, men who wanted nothing more than a chance to add to their regimental legacies tracing back to Waterloo and beyond.

You could ask yourself: 'Did the Junta really think their soldiers could beat the British?'

My answer to that would be no. I think the whole thing was a bluff. They didn't ever think that we would go to war over the Falklands, and if we did, they must have reckoned that the Americans would put a muzzle on us.

Not only did the Junta underestimate the resolve of the British people and its politicians, but they had made the gamble at a time that was already precarious for them. Argentina and Chile were involved in a dispute over the Beagle Channel, a strait at the extreme southern tip of South America between Chile and Argentina. As a result, Chile was marshalling troops close to the Argentine border. Argentina countered this threat by redeploying three of their best brigades, including one of paratroopers and two mountain warfare brigades – soldiers who would be much better trained and adapted to fighting in the inhospitable conditions of the Falklands.

Argentina is a huge country with a variety of topography and many of its troops had been trained to fight in jungle conditions. Inexplicably, those men made up a lot of the soldiers sent to fight in a South Atlantic winter.

Argentinian men were expected to do a year of national service and in 1982 that duty befell those born in 1963. Their basic training began in February 1982 and as a consequence, the conscripts were especially green when the British fleet set sail. No doubt many of these young men felt a fierce sense of national pride as well as a sense of duty and I imagine that many of them were naturally gifted soldiers who would have excelled under the right tutelage but you simply cannot expect near-amateurs to compete with professionals. I don't say any of this to undermine the bravery of character of these men, but simply to point out that training matters and we had it over them in spades.

The enemy could, however, outnumber us (and did). Argentina had eight infantry brigades available at the beginning of the war in 1982 and we were sailing south with two. Given the ratio for attackers should be 3:1, we were on the back foot numerically, even if they deployed the bare minimum.

Royal Navy submariners have to be given credit for saving many British lives. Once Argentina realised that Britain meant business, and was heading south for war, the Junta began to reinforce the garrison on the islands. This was especially needed because, believing that Britain would not choose to fight, the Junta had withdrawn many of their forces after the initial invasion. Thanks to the threat posed by British submarines that had arrived in the area, the Argentinians could not risk reinforcing the islands by ship. Instead, all of their men and equipment had to come via the air into the airfield at Port Stanley. Not only did this greatly slow the speed at which they could reinforce, but it also meant that very little heavy equipment could be brought in.

If you can believe it, the enemy leaders sent the 3rd (Jungle) Infantry Brigade to fight on an island that barely has any trees, let alone a canopy. Many of this unit were conscripts or reservists (recently released conscripts) who were called back into service.

The 10th Mechanised Infantry Brigade was given the area around Port Stanley. They were equipped with some armoured cars, but for the most part they were on foot – or more accurately, waiting in fighting positions.

As well as these infantry brigades, the Argentinian Army also deployed artillery and cavalry (armoured cars) to the islands. They were joined there by more than a battalion of Marines and smaller units that one finds in any army, such as medical staff, intelligence teams and so on. There were also Argentine special forces on the islands, as I would come to learn first-hand.

Land forces aside, the enemy possessed an impressive aerial threat and a credible one at sea. They would be no pushover, we knew, but I don't think we wanted them to be. I can only speak for myself, but I had joined the army to be challenged: I had found that in peace, now I wanted to find it in war.

* * *

There was no moping about in the wake of the helicopter crash. We would honour our fallen brothers the best way we knew how – by fighting for them.

G Squadron's patrols were slowly exfiltrating and rejoining the fleet. They'd lived in the harsh rain and cold for weeks and it must have been a blow to them to get back to the ship only to find out that some of their mates had died on the Sea King. After a few days to eat hot food and get some rest, they'd be back out on ops. Without doubt, I know that they wanted to get involved in the direct-action missions – what soldier wouldn't?

It appeared as though our task for now would be in creating diversions and sewing confusion across the enemy force. To create as much chaos as possible, and make our presence felt across the army, we broke down into half-troop elements, or at times, even smaller.

A troop should consist of 16 men, but my own troop was 14 – very rarely were the squadrons fully manned, even before battlefield casualties. This was because there were always some injuries in training that required rehabilitation, people would be away attending courses like Senior Brecon, or perhaps detached on some other kind of work, such as instructing or clandestine. Our boss had an infantry background, as did our troop sergeant. The junior ranks were a mix of Paras, line infantry and rifles, but we also had a cook from the navy. Move over, Steven Seagal in the US thriller *Under Siege*, we had the original special forces chef!

We were armed with a variety of small arms, mostly the M16 with 203mm grenade launcher, the 7.62mm belt-fed General Purpose Machine Gun (GPMG) and Browning HP pistols. We also carried a variety of grenades, including high-explosive, phosphorus and smoke.

I carried an M16, but I would come to regret it. The weapon uses a 5.56mm round and like most of my comrades, I'd come to wish I had the Self-Loading Rifle (SLR). Like the GPMG, it fired a 7.62mm round, which carried a lot more stopping power. The SLR was well suited for this campaign and I was glad that our infantry battalions had such a solid weapon. As well as our small arms, our troop would carry the limited amount of Stinger anti-aircraft missiles we'd been given, courtesy of Delta Force. Training on them was limited to say the least, but he who dares wins!

The time had come to leave the *Intrepid*, which I think all of us were glad of. That's no slight against her crew, but I would forever associate the *Intrepid*'s flight deck with the Sea King crash. That was where we had seen the heli's navigation light disappear; that was from where we had watched the search for our brothers; where I had held the dead crewman's hand. And where we were told that the regiment should be seen to be taking casualties. I didn't have any good memories on board that ship and I was glad to be heading for land. There was an enemy waiting for us, of course, but there was a certain helplessness as a soldier aboard the ships. If the Argentinian bombs and missiles came for us, there was nothing we could do but watch and pray that the pilots missed.

We lifted off from *Intrepid*'s flight deck in 864 Squadron's Sea Kings. Of course, flying in a helicopter for the first time after the crash was a weird experience. I'd always loved Sea Kings, and helis in general, and though there was no hesitation from anyone getting on board, the usual sense of jubilation that you get when going on a mission wasn't there either. It felt good to be moving, though. Good to be advancing towards the enemy and in a direct-action role no less.

There was a risk of enemy aircraft and so we flew low across the ground and hoped that the Sea Harriers in their combat air patrols would shield us. Then, the helicopter's wheels touched down on the ground and I jumped down onto the wet earth of the Falkland Islands.

As I looked around me, for a moment I almost thought that I was on Sennybridge Training Area in Wales! Other than the absence of forestry blocks, the places looked identical – rugged, windswept moorlands and the clumped bushy reeds known to squaddies as 'babies' heads'. Brecon was home to the infantryman and somewhere British soldiers practised section attacks to perfection. It was our bread and butter, what we did best. We'd soon find out if the Argentinians had trained as hard and as well as we had done.

Somehow I doubted it.

After the Sea King took off, we shouldered our heavy bergens and moved off silently across the boggy ground, careful to avoid silhouetting ourselves on high ground – known as 'skylining'. We took regular pauses to stop and listen. In this kind of terrain, you'll often hear something before you see it – a careless voice is easily carried in the wind, not to mention the cocking of a machine gun's handle, which might signal that you just walked into an ambush.

The target for our patrol was a small house and outbuildings on an inlet close to Darwin. As we approached, we gave Goose Green a wide berth. G Squadron had reported a large number of the enemy there, something 2 Para would soon confirm in the most violent of fashions, as they would be the battalion tasked with taking it.

Our troop boss gathered us together in dead ground out of sight from the enemy and gave confirmatory orders. The first order of business was to confirm if the target house was empty or not, but we could not confirm this from 200 metres. There was no sign of light and the strong wind that came in our direction carried no sound of voices, or the smell of food, or smoke. Still, we had come to create a diversion and create one we would. The boss gave the order to open fire and tracers began to stream across the open ground. All of a sudden the quiet night had been turned into a racket and there was no way the action could have been missed by the enemy. No fire was coming back our way, however, and it seemed we had tabbed through the night to shoot up an empty building!

Oh well, mission accomplished. We saw the funny side and I could hear laughter all around me. We waited a while for an enemy that would not appear. Disappointed, we faded away into the night.

A word to young soldiers: just because you don't think what you're doing is important, doesn't mean that it isn't. That night I had laughed and felt pissed off that we had come all that way to shoot up an empty house, but we would later find out that the diversion had worked and worked well. Prisoners of war would tell us that their commanders thought that the main force had already landed and it was they who were engaging targets that night. Because of that, the actual landing at San Carlos caught them unaware. As the great strategist Sun Tsu once said: all war is based on deception.

The other troops had also opened fire on their own targets and with mixed results. One patrol had captured an enemy soldier and a trooper stepped forwards to interrogate him in Spanish. Perhaps he had missed a few lessons on the course because the Argentinian later wondered why he'd been questioned about food and not his unit! That cracked us all up. Even more so when we learned that it was Mobility Troop who were once again providing the giggles.

On the heels of our diversions, landing craft began to put men and material ashore at San Carlos.

Despite the daring attempts of the Argentinian pilots there was no stopping the fleet and the task to stop our infantry would fall to theirs. The shore at San Carlos was under the protection of a group of Argentinians from their 25th Infantry Group, commanded by Lieutenant Carlos Esteban. To his credit, the officer positioned his unit of approximately 60 men on a position at Fanning Head where they could observe the sound and hit the landing craft with recoilless rifles and mortar. When the landings began, Lieutenant Esteban had his men open fire, but they were soon silenced by naval gunfire and a counterattack by a sizeable troop from the Special Boat Service. The enemy didn't go down without a fight, with 11 men killed. They also shot down two Gazelle helicopters flying at low level – three of the four crew were killed.

Blue Beach was the first landing site at San Carlos and here, 40 Commando, 2 Para and 3 Commando Brigade Headquarters arrived first. In the next phase of landings at Red Beach, Ajax Bay, 45 Commando came ashore, along with artillery and logistics. The third phase was at Port San Carlos, known as Green Beach, and this was where 42 Commando, 3 Para and more support arms got their boots on dry land. I say 'dry', but that is a relative term in a place like the Falklands!

The Royal Navy and army logisticians should take a bow as it is no mean feat to land 2,400 men ashore with their supplies and all of this under enemy air attack. To counter the air threat, 12 Rapier air defence systems were landed, but they proved to be ineffective – apparently, the distance of travel from Britain had affected their targeting systems and they'd prove largely useless at downing enemy aircraft. It didn't help that most of their spare parts were at the bottom of the ocean on board the *Atlantic Conveyor*, but I imagine that the sight and presence of them did something to deter the enemy. The Royal Navy's Sea Dart missile system seemed more capable and would account for seven enemy aircraft destroyed during the campaign.

It was a tough few days for the Royal Navy, though they rose to the occasion admirably. As well as losing the HMS *Ardent* and HMS *Antelope* at San Carlos, HMS *Broadsword*,

HMS *Argonaut*, HMS *Brilliant* and HMS *Antrim* were also damaged, mostly by cannon fire.

On 24 May, the enemy pilots changed their attention away from the warships and to the transport vessels carrying men and supplies. RFA *Sir Bedivere*, *Sir Galahad* and *Sir Lancelot* were all damaged by bombs – it was the *Lancelot* that had carried me across the water for my first tour in Northern Ireland and so I was particularly aggrieved to hear that she'd been hit. Tragically, there was much worse to come for the *Sir Galahad*.

For the infantry on the shore, the first thing they had to do was dig in – a time-honoured part of war that they took to with gusto. The Argentinians possessed mortar and artillery and the best defence an infantryman had against them was to get below ground. I imagine they would have felt like they were back on Sennybridge Training Area if not for the sight of San Carlos water behind them and the massive cacophony of noise as enemy aircraft roared in to attack our ships and gunfire and missiles rose up to greet them. It was a good thing the infantry were fast workers with their spades, because the Argentine air force soon turned their attention to them! Footage of these attacks often made it onto the news and I imagine it was just as terrifying for a family back home to watch as it was to be on the receiving end of it.

A vitally important field hospital was set up in an abandoned warehouse at Ajax Bay. Casualties from both sides were treated there and captured Argentinian doctors and medics were allowed to work freely alongside their British counter-parts. Once the wounded had been stabilised, they were taken to the fleet's hospital ship, the SS *Canberra*. The commander of the field hospital was Rick Jolly (RN), who would later write a book about the 'Red and Green Life Machine',* as the field hospital came to be known. I'm sure a lot of people owe him their lives. He died in 2018, aged 71.

A total of 18 x 105mm light guns had been brought to the campaign, these artillery pieces belonging to 29 Commando. Of course, a gun is only as good as its ammunition and ammo dumps began to be set up across the landing area.

With the loss of the *Atlantic Conveyor* and the Chinook heli-copters it was carrying, much of the small-arms ammunition and mortar rounds would need to be carried in the bergens of the infantry. The *Atlantic Conveyor* had also been transporting a total of 14 Sea Harriers and GR3s, which would have signif-icantly increased our chances of air superiority and close air support. As it was, the boots on the ground could expect to be on the end of minefields, small arms fire, artillery, mortars, bombings and strafing runs – not to mention the Falklands weather, which can be lethal in itself!

Our infantry force would be operating in two brigades: 3 Commando and 5 Brigade. As the two consolidated ashore there was a period of inactivity for D Squadron, but not our

---

* *The Red and Green Life Machine: A Diary of the Falklands Field Hospital*, Rick Jolly, Century, 1983.

planners. Thankfully, B Squadron's suicide mission to Tierra del Fuego seemed to be permanently scrapped and their men began to arrive at the task force in dribs and drabs. They were brought in by sub or flown down from Ascension before parachuting into the ocean – if you're going to arrive late at a party, arrive in style!

Although the plan to land on the enemy's runway at Tierra del Fuego had been scrapped, the Exocet threat was still massive and not out of our planners' minds. One morning in June, the residents of Punta Arenas, Chile, woke to find the burnt-out wreckage of a Sea King on a sandbank. Three British crewmen gave themselves up and told the Chilean authorities that they'd got lost in bad weather and had to crash-land their aircraft. Something didn't add up, but it wasn't until the nineties that the story came out...

The Sea King had been flying half a troop of SAS soldiers to Tierra del Fuego. Their mission was to establish an OP that could report on activity from the Argentinian air base – such early warning could put the Sea Harriers in position to intercept the incoming ship destroyers and take the Super Etendards and their Exocets off the board for good.

Due to flying well beyond its range, it was always going to be a one-way trip, but the plan had been to ditch the Sea King at sea so that the infiltration remained a secret. For whatever reason, the pilot and patrol commander could not confirm where they were supposed to land and so they decided to ditch the heli in Chile and extract back to the task force through the backdoor, rather than fulfilling the mission. Chile was chosen as the extraction route because they had their own sabre rattling with Argentina and there were British agents there in place to see our men home after the mission. Personally, I think the heli should have been ditched where they could and then tabbed into Argentina and on to the target. I don't see why the mission was scrubbed just because they had a longer distance to cover – we do selection for a reason.

Not only was the mission abandoned, but the Sea King was dumped on a sandbank, rather than in deep water that could have hidden it. Perhaps this was down to bad luck and a high tide, but either way, it was an incredibly embarrassing moment for the regiment.

Back in the UK, little of the Special Boat Service's activities were being reported on the news and I want to give them their credit here. The 'Shakies' were involved in the initial intelligence gathering alongside G Squadron and they were vital in the beach recces, which included searching for underwater objects/booby traps that would destroy landing craft.

The SBS also planned two operations against targets on the Argentinian mainland: one was planned against an airfield, the other against a harbour believed to be receiving more Exocets from our great allies, the French. In the end neither operation was launched. They were incredibly risky and with the end of the war drawing closer, I suppose the risk wasn't deemed to justify the potential reward.

I understand that it sounds like a lot of hubris when I say the war was coming to an end when we'd only just started landing our troops. We were yet to dislodge the enemy from the positions that they'd had almost two months to prepare, but neither I nor my comrades were ever in doubt that we'd win. Once we got the infantry ashore, it was a matter of when, and not if, we would end the war with Britain victorious. Argentina's one chance had been in her air power and Exocets. If they could have done to us what the *Conqueror* did to the *Belgrano*, perhaps the British public would have said that 'the price is too high'.

To be quite honest, I'm not sure if that would even have been the case. Britain was in the grips of patriotism and that is a powerful and often unstoppable force. When combined with one of the most highly trained militaries in world history, I just didn't see how the enemy could stand against us.

* * *

Sometimes it felt like the enemy wasn't even on the islands. D Squadron launched a number of missions to engage the enemy, but we kept coming up empty-handed. However, all was not in vain. We'd brought the Stinger anti-aircraft missiles ashore on our diversionary raids and Kiwi spotted an enemy Pucará aircraft! As you might have guessed, Kiwi was from New Zealand and he had been recruited to 22 SAS by one of the troop's corporals, Karl, during an exercise in that country. New Zealand and Australia have their own SAS, but it's not unusual for men from the Commonwealth to serve in the British forces. Kiwi was best known for his skydiving, where he would jump with his black Labrador strapped to his chest. Seeing that Lab's ears flapping in the wind always brought a smile to our faces, but today, Kiwi was looking to shoot down a plane, not jump out of one. The Stinger missiles were supposed to be fired at the rear of an aircraft so that they could get a good heat source from the engine outlet, but Kiwi decided to take a shot head-on so he aimed, paused and let fire. It shot through the sky and hit the target dead-on. We all cheered – brilliant! The plane went down and the pilot ejected. I found out he was then captured, but later, as it was not by us.

That was our first experience with Stingers and Pucarás. Our second came on 28 May. Out of sight to us, the men of 2 Para had advanced on the Argentinian positions at Goose Green, a name that would become familiar in British homes and a battle I will cover in more detail shortly. For now, let me just say that 2 Para were heavily engaged, but all we could see of it were two Pucarás which appeared in the distance in a patrol formation. Corporal Karl picked up a Stinger and decided to have a crack at the pilot if they got closer to the Lying Up Position (LUP).

Sure enough they did and Karl shouldered the weapon, reckoned he had it locked on the Pucará and then fired. The missile flew a pathetically short distance and hit the ground. All that he'd done was to leave a huge cloud of smoke to mark our position, while the two aircraft remained totally untouched – *shit!*

Not one to give up easily, Karl picked up a second Stinger, aimed and fired. For a second time the missile landed harmlessly in the dirt and we had left a second cloud of smoke for the enemy pilots to spot. This time, the pilots did not miss it.

The attack planes turned towards us like sharks in the sky – *shit!*

My heart was in my mouth. They knew where we were and there was no outrunning them. Thoughts flashed through my mind – what were they armed with? Rockets? Cannons? Napalm? It was the thought of that burning fuel that worried me the most. As far as death goes, I couldn't think of a worse way to go than napalm.

I looked at a few of the other lads. No one was smiling, but no one looked panicked, either: what was done was done. It was pointless running, we'd never get away from them, and so the best we could hope for was to get low and maybe put the pilots off their attack run with small arms. As I knelt in the wet ground and aimed my rifle up, I didn't believe for one second that my 5.56mm rounds would do anything against the aircraft, but the only other option was to do nothing and I at least wanted to go down fighting.

I looked down the barrel of my rifle at the two planes drawing closer in the sky, the sound of their engines growing louder and louder. *At what point would they open fire? At what point would we?* I was waiting for that order when I spotted the miracle: 'Their rocket pods are empty!' I shouted. 'They've got no rockets!'

As clear as day, I could see the black recesses in the pods beneath the Pucará's wings. They must have been out of cannon ammunition too because they didn't fire their cannon either, instead just buzzing overhead and out of sight. They must have dumped everything onto the Paras at Goose Green and I can only guess that they turned towards us for the same reason that our ships turned towards an Exocet – it made for a more difficult target.

Whatever the case, both we and the pilots lived to fight another day.

In the distance, the battle of Goose Green raged on and many men would not be so lucky.

* * *

Perhaps the task force commanders at the time had not been reading their Sun Tsu, because on the morning of 28 May 1982, a BBC broadcast announced to all of the world that 2 Para were on their way to assault the enemy forces at Goose Green: with friends like that, who needs enemies?

The paratroopers in question were going up against an estimated 650–1,000 enemy troops, but not all of them were combatants. A full-strength British infantry battalion at the time was 650, but that includes all parts of the supply and command chain. The Paras would be outnumbered, but knowing them, they probably enjoyed that – after all, the worse the odds, the better the story.

It was essential that the enemy force at Goose Green be neutralised for one very simple reason: with that strength, and in striking distance of San Carlos, they could cause serious disruption to the task force's landing sites in and around that settlement. In order to prevent that from happening, 2 Para would need to kill or capture all of the Argentinian soldiers on the narrow isthmus. It was not good enough just to force the enemy from the battlefield, allowing them to regroup later: they must be fixed and destroyed, one way or another.

There was no fancy way of doing this. Like the battlefields of Waterloo and Normandy, the infantry would form up in companies and advance to contact. Then, engaged by the enemy, they would have to keep pushing forwards through the enemy's fire, taking out defensive position after position until all of the enemy were either dead or under the white flag of truce.

Nasty, hard business, but that's war.

Although the Argentinian force at Goose Green was a strong one, within striking distance, I've never believed that they could have pushed us back into the sea. Perhaps I'm biased, but I just don't believe the British troops ashore would have given up that ground. No doubt there was a danger of disruption, but once we got a single pair of boots on the island, I think the Argentinians were on borrowed time. As I say, I may be biased, but nothing that I saw in the war made me believe that they could go toe-to-toe with us, let alone drive us out of defensive positions that would be supported with naval gunfire support.

Like anything, there are pros and cons to being an assaulting or a defending force. Defenders can lose their nerve because they feel stuck in position and worry about what's happening on their flanks and behind them. It can be hard on the nerves, particularly for conscripts. Being on the attack gives you a certain belief – real or not – that you are more in control of a situation because you are on the offensive and when you take one objective, it builds momentum to take the next. In defence, you're playing a deadly game of whack a mole, where you're constantly waiting for the next enemy to pop up, and all the time they're getting closer and closer. Imagine what it must feel like for a conscript soldier in his trench once the British infantry gets so close he can hear them shouting orders and raising blood-curdling screams as they drive their bayonets home into his comrades. The loud crump of grenades signals another bunker cleared. *Are the Brits behind you? Flanking you? Will you even see them before you die?*

No wonder so many of them surrendered. It would have been tough for experienced soldiers, let alone those who had been civilians only a few months before. That did not mean that they did not put up a stiff fight, however. In fact, an Argentinian chaplain noted the different attitudes in the conscript companies. He said that one company fought because they had to and another did so because they wanted glory. In his eyes, both were equally brave.

The fighting in Goose Green kicked off in the early hours of the morning with a naval bombardment courtesy of HMS *Arrow*. She fired illumination and high explosives and this was 2 Para's cover to begin moving into the attack. Unfortunately, the naval gunfire support was ineffective and did not smash the enemy positions, nor their spirit, but A Company managed to take their first objective without casualties. It was a house that turned out to be occupied by Falklanders, not the enemy. A Company were in a favourable position to press on, but were told to hold.

B Company began to push onto the isthmus on which Goose Green was located. There were exchanges of gunfire, but nothing deadly.

D Company began to advance between B and A. They came under heavy fire from a machine gun, but this position was assaulted and cleared by two brave paratroopers. This allowed D Company to put in an attack on the platoon-strength enemy holding Coronation Ridge. They were successful in doing so, but it came at a price: three Paras were killed.

Artillery and mortar fire onto A Company's positions held them up from pushing on. Despite already being wounded, a brave Argentinian officer was controlling the fire onto A Company and stopping them from advancing. He was finally killed by a sniper's bullet and later decorated for his actions –

and rightly so, in my opinion. Bravery is bravery, no matter whose flag you're fighting under.

The fight for Darwin Hill became a real scrap between A Company and the belligerent Argentinian defence. As the early hours gave way to daylight, this meant that the Argie machine gunners had the high ground and good visibility to pick their targets. In the face of this wall of fire, the attack became bogged down.

Lieutenant Colonel Harry 'H' Jones was the commanding officer of 2 Para and at this point he decided that the initiative had been surrendered to the enemy and must be regained if 2 Para were to be victorious. 'H' Jones charged an enemy position in a gulley and three of his men that followed him were killed. Jones attempted to attack an Argentinian trench but was shot before he could make it. A Scout helicopter was called in to evacuate him, but this was shot down by an Argentinian Pucará aircraft. The Scout's pilot was killed and the co-pilot severely wounded.

There appear to be two schools of thought when it comes to 'H' Jones's actions. One is that he was a brave man and worthy of the Victoria Cross he would receive posthumously, after he died of his wounds. The other is that he was a fool who got other men killed in a personal quest for glory and that his death only further bogged down the attack as the entire battalion's command structure then needed to be reshuffled.

I fall somewhere in the middle. I have no doubt that Jones was a brave man and it's not for me to say what was going on in his head at the time. Perhaps it was all for personal glory, or maybe he really did think it was the best way to get the attack going forwards. Who knows?

In the aftermath of Jones's death, A Company made a third attempt to take the ridge, but this also failed. It's supposed to be the defenders who are fixed and destroyed, but with the assault so bogged down, 2 Para were now in a very dangerous position and it is fair to say that their mortar platoon played a huge part in keeping them in the fight: 1,000 rounds were fired onto the enemy positions, causing casualties and keeping their heads down. But the enemy had their own supporting assets and called in a flight of Argentinian A4 Skyhawks. This was a nightmare scenario for the British infantry: pinned down by machine gun and sniper fire, they were sitting ducks for enemy bombs and strafing runs.

Thankfully, 'the fog of war' came into play here and in favour of the British. Not only did the Skyhawks arrive late and low on fuel, but they fired on Argentine positions and Argentine air defence weapons fired on them, damaging the lead aircraft. It was a win-win for the Paras!

2 Para would not give up and finally cleared Darwin Ridge almost 12 hours after HMS *Arrow* began the attack with its naval bombardment. By then, 2 Para had been fighting for almost six hours and had lost 12 men, including the CO and adjutant, and Goose Green was still not taken.

2 Para had a true battle on its hands.

* * *

Now that Darwin Ridge was under British ownership, the next step was to take the airfield at Goose Green.

The enemy had 35mm anti-aircraft guns that they began firing directly at the advancing Paras, causing terrible wounds and killing several men. Despite this storm of fire, the Paras would not be stopped and as the Argentinian positions began to fall, many of the enemy began to surrender.

It was now that an infamous incident occurred. Some witnesses claim that when British soldiers went forward to accept a surrender under truce of a white flag, they were shot by Argentinian soldiers, with one killed outright. The second Brit was hit in the knee and then finished off at point-blank range with a shot to the head.

I wasn't there, so I don't know if that's how it happened, or if it happened at all. All I can say is that you hear stories at war and some of them stick with you more than others. That one has stayed with me.

As the fight went on, British Harriers raided the airfield and the Paras were on the receiving end of attacks from Pucarás. The enemy aircraft suffered losses, including one which was allegedly carrying napalm: canisters and supplies of which were later found at the airfield. There is no such thing as a nice injury in war, but there's something particularly sinister about a jelly-like fuel that sticks to your skin and melts away at your flesh. If you're lucky, the napalm will kill you quickly, but many victims are simply stripped of skin and flesh and die of the infections that usually follow such a massive trauma.

As last light fell, 2 Para were still in a fight and had not secured the day's objectives. To make matters worse, enemy helicopters were flying in reserves, taken from Mount Kent – a decision by the enemy that would later play into our hands. British helicopters also ferried in support, including Royal Marines – which I can only think was a delight for them and a sore spot for the Paras – and took out casualties.

That night, Argentinian prisoners of war (POWs) were sent back to their lines, still fighting in Goose Green, with terms for surrender. The Argentinian forces had put up a strong defence, but they were surrounded and held out no hope of reinforcement. To continue would have meant a bombardment of the civilian settlements to root them out and to their enemy's credit, they made the honourable decision to surrender rather than prolong the fighting and cause unnecessary damage to the area.

The next morning, after burning the regimental flag so that it would not be taken as a trophy, the enemy laid down their weapons and surrendered. The Battle of Goose Green was over. It had cost the British forces: 18 men killed and 64 wounded. The enemy losses were about twice that, with more than 900 men also captured. A bloody day on the islands, it would not be the last.

* * *

The SAS can't do its job alone. We needed the RAF to get us to Ascension and the Royal Fleet Auxiliary and Royal Navy to get us from there to the Falklands. Once in the South Atlantic,

RAF and Fleet Air Arm pilots shuttled us on helicopters. If we were wounded, it would be doctors, nurses and surgeons from across the services who would work on us.

What was true on the task force level was also true in the regiment. To become a member of 22 SAS, and join a sabre squadron, a soldier had to complete special forces selection – also known as becoming 'badged'. However, there were also attached personnel in the regiment who were 'non-badged'. We couldn't function without them. If you think of a sports team, you have the guys on the pitch and then support staff on the sidelines and more again in the offices. That's pretty much what it's like in the regiment. The badged guys are on the field, the 'non-badged' helping us to do our jobs in other roles. It takes all of us to make a success of our missions.

We had a rule in the regiment that non-badged personnel would not go out on the ground and for good reason – you're only as strong as your weakest link. Realistically, if they had what it takes to be special forces soldiers, then they would have gone to selection and got badged.

One of the key roles for the non-badged was signals. Although we were all trained to a certain degree, these guys were the experts. We always had a badged signaller working with them – on one patrol, our officer commanding was talked into taking a non-badged signaller with him. This was because our badged signaller reckoned that the lad was 'badged material,' and wanted the OC to try him out.

It was a bad idea. The signaller struggled to carry his load over the terrain and couldn't keep up with the OC. They were alone on the ground together and the OC decided that the only option was to cache – essentially meaning to hide – the signaller's bergan and come back for it at a later point in the patrol. This surprised a lot of us when we found out, because the non-badged signaller had come to us from the Paras. You don't get into that regiment without a good attitude and good fitness, and we could only guess that once on the ground – and operating with just our squadron commander Cedric Delves for company – the signaller had got the wind up him and the failure had come in his mind, not his body. This guess seemed to be backed up by the fact that he moved quickly enough once he saw the extraction point! Physical fitness is just one aspect of what makes a special forces soldier. What's between the ears and behind the ribs matters too. It doesn't matter how far you can run, or how many pull-ups you can do. If your head and heart isn't in the fight, you're no use to the special forces.

At the end of the mission, the OC found the badged signaller and told him curtly: 'He is not badged material.' So that was that and the young pretender was returned to his unit at the end of the war.

It had been a bad day for the OC and it was about to get much worse. His friend of old, Lieutenant Colonel 'H' Jones, had been killed during 2 Para's attack at Goose Green. 'Colonel H' would be posthumously awarded the Victoria Cross for his actions. The Paras had had a hell of a fight on their hands and secured a hard-fought victory in what could be considered the first proper infantry engagement of the war.

There were many more to come.

* * *

D squadron was taken off the ground, this time onto HMS *Fearless*, an amphibious landing ship where the regimental HQ was situated and sister ship to the *Intrepid*. We would not be on board for long, however.

We had a new mission.

Mount Kent lay on the Commando and Infantry Brigade's route to Port Stanley. At the moment, there was no heavy presence of the enemy there, but the landing at San Carlos had taken them by surprise and they had not reinforced the heights after pulling the company off them to reinforce Goose Green. Now that the enemy knew where we had come ashore, they could make a good guess at what our routes would be and no doubt would heavily occupy the slopes of Mount Kent – so we had to get there first.

Loaded up onto the Sea Kings, we flew forwards of the brigade and onto the high ground more than 60 kilometres away from the nearest infantry. As we disembarked onto the windswept mountainside, one thing became very clear: we were on our own.

With the *Atlantic Conveyor* and the Chinooks at the bottom of the ocean, the infantry would have to tab their way across

East Falkland in order to join us. We'd be waiting for days, at least, and so we began to disperse among the rocks at the top of the slopes. For now, they were our concealment; if the enemy came, they'd become our fighting positions.

Along with Mobility, Air Troop set up on the eastern slope of the mountain. We used rocks to build a mortar pit so that the base plate wouldn't sink as it had done on Pebble Island. After that, there was nothing to do but watch and wait.

The next morning, nine enemy helicopters flew out of Port Stanley and came right over our positions. We'd later learn that they were carrying a full company of troops, but at the time all we could see were the airframes. They were absolute sitting ducks and there's no doubt we could have brought down several of them with a mixture of rockets, Stingers and small arms fire. However, our orders were to remain unseen. It was the right decision because we didn't want to let the enemy know we had occupied the mountain and allow them to attack us before we could reinforce, but I don't think I've ever been more frustrated in my life. It was the kind of target that a soldier dreams of and we had to watch and let it go – I doubt those on board ever knew how close they came to death that day.

The first onto the mountain after us were two airlifted 105mm guns of 29 Commando, Royal Artillery. They were the first of six that would be placed on Mount Kent, where they would be able to provide invaluable fire support onto the several mountains separating us from Port Stanley and victory. D Squadron was to provide support for the gunners until the infantry arrived and they positioned themselves within our perimeter.

Also arriving with the 105s was Colonel Rose and he had a guest. We were sitting in our mortar pit when a comical face appeared over the stone wall that we'd built around it. The man was wearing Colonel Blimp* glasses, a First World War-era Tommy helmet and his face was black with cam (camouflage) cream: 'Any spare weapons here, chaps?' he asked in that quintessential British accent, then introduced himself as Max Hastings – a correspondent who would become known as the foremost authority on the war.

He seemed like a nice enough bloke and we asked him what he was doing up on Mount Kent with Colonel Rose. It turned out that Max had made a deal – he was in possession of a satellite phone and the regiment was not. Our colonel could use the phone to talk directly with the brigadier back in the UK and I expect that what the war correspondent got in return was access to the SAS. I also have no doubt that he was a patriot and wanted Britain to be successful in a campaign that was far from over. I'm sure he would have loaned the phone regardless, but there's nothing wrong with using a little leverage to get a good scoop!

Mr Hastings left our mortar pit in search of more stories. He became a leading authority on the conflict and has played

---

* A British cartoon character created by David Low in 1934.

an important part in keeping it in the public eye since the end of the war. For that, he has my thanks and I'm sorry that we didn't have any weapons to spare!

* * *

Troops from 42 Commando began to arrive at Mount Kent and the regiment acted as guides to lead them towards Mount Harriet, the most westerly of the mountains that would need to be cleared of the enemy.

More and more companies of infantry began to pass through, the men having completed the arduous march across almost the entire width of the island. They looked exhausted, but undaunted and ready to close with the enemy. You had to take your hat off to them – *good luck, lads!*

There's always something powerful about seeing a unit moving up for an attack. I've witnessed it in several wars, against several enemies, but the look of the infantry soldier is always the same. It's a determined look, with a hard set to the eyes. As they move up to the battle, even the jokers fall silent. Some smoke a final cigarette, others share water. Some of these men will kill. Some will be killed. All of them will be changed forever.

Here's to the infantryman.

* * *

One night, as near pitch-dark was settling over the island, we observed two 'Huey' helicopters disembarking troops at the bottom of the mountain. We missed the opportunity to take down the American-made aircraft with an American-made anti-aircraft missile – you have to love the arms industry! – but planned on laying on a welcome for the section strength of enemy (about eight men) who were surely here to come up the mountain and attack our positions.

The obvious covered route for them to use was a gully that came up the mountain from where they had disembarked and so we moved quickly down the mountain to set up an L-shaped ambush.

I was in the cut-off group with an experienced corporal, Yorkie. We set up and waited for our prey, but suddenly a massive contact kicked off on our left, the night erupting into noise and the flash of tracers. The rest of the troop had made contact with the enemy before properly setting in the ambush and rounds started to hit the rocks surrounding us.

I asked Yorkie if he could see the enemy. We only had one pair of night vision goggles (NVGs) and now he used them to spot the Argentinians as they started running back down from the hill.

'Spot me,' I said and fired a 40mm grenade down the mountain. It exploded with a flash in the dark and Yorkie gave me adjustments. I had to move the weapon out of the aim to reload, so it wasn't the most accurate way to fight, but I was having fun. If we put some illumination up, it would have been a different story, but the decision was made not to put the parachute flares into the sky, I imagine because we were still trying to conceal our numbers on the mountain and illumination works both ways.

I wanted to see the enemy and so I took the NVGs from Yorkie and he started firing instead. We kept firing until they were out of range and I couldn't stop giggling when the enemy would jump out of cover and run like they were in a Laurel and Hardy movie.

The contact went on for some time, but once the enemy had pulled back and disappeared into the night, we went down the slope to investigate. Their patrol had been quick to dump their kit and we found NVGs and cold weather clothing, which we distributed among ourselves. I ended up with a parka coat, which was lovely and warm – I didn't even care that it was covered in blood, it would do me for the rest of the campaign. The individual's ID card was in the pocket – I still have it today, but I can't say I ever returned his coat.

We had three of our own injured in the fight. Karl and Dick both had shrapnel wounds, but nothing critical. Digger had broken his hand and so I placed a back slab (a splint of sorts) on it to hold it firm. With the lads patched up and the enemy's kit pilfered, we went back up the mountain but the action wasn't over.

Three of the enemy breached Boat Troop's perimeter and started lobbing grenades. They caused one light casualty and paid for it with their lives – Boat Troop's grenade throwing turned out to be more accurate and all three of the enemy were killed. Brave men, in my opinion.

I didn't see their bodies, or their burial, but I know it would have been conducted with respect. We didn't hate the enemy. They were soldiers like us, only we were better, and it was they who died for their country that night. As for our wounded, they caught a helicopter flight out in the morning, but all returned to us before the end of the campaign. We were undermanned already and the lads did not want to miss out on any action.

That night was the first of five attempts by the enemy's special forces to attack us on Mount Kent. Of the estimated 50 men that were sent against us, 32 were either killed or wounded in action. Attacking high ground is a dangerous proposition at the best of times; attacking the SAS on high ground is tantamount to suicide.

During one attack, Boat Troop took one of the enemy captive. A big man, he paced around aggressively once he had been disarmed of his sporting rifle and dumdum ammunition (banned under the Geneva Conventions). Because of the grooved head of these bullets they 'explode' on impact, rather than passing through flesh like a solid bullet does. Flattening the top of a bullet has a similar devastating effect and it is against the law for a soldier to tamper with his bullets in any way.

The OC had a word with him and whatever he said must have worked – the soldier sat down and remained very sullen and very quiet until he was taken away for interrogation.

More and more of the infantry passed by the mountain. Our time on Mount Kent was coming to an end, but I had something to do before we left…

The 105mm guns had been firing at the Argentinian positions on the other mountains and I helped myself to four of the empty shells – two would later become umbrella stands and the other two I had made into ashtrays. I hadn't come all this way to go home empty-handed!

We didn't know it then, but a few members of the artillery gunners on Mount Kent would become friends of mine in later years. Two would go on selection and one would eventually command D Squadron before returning to 29 Commando as their commanding officer. I'd even work with one of the gents decades later, as a civilian contractor in the UAE. We remain friends to this day.

* * *

We left Mount Kent after about a week on the heights, flown to our new forward operating base (FOB), the RFA *Sir Lancelot* – as I've said, this was the vessel that had carried me on my first tour to Northern Ireland and a lot had happened to us both since then. *Lancelot* had been damaged by a bomb, but she was intact and seaworthy, and standing alone in San Carlos Water. The crewmen of the vessel were Hong Chinese from Hong Kong, and though they had been offered the chance to leave the ship at Ascension, they had stayed on with their British officers. To me that speaks volumes not only of their loyalty, but of the leadership of the ship's officers.

Our next mission was to insert onto West Falkland to check out a small house on the waterline. Our small team was taken in via Sea King with no problems. As usual, the South Atlantic wind was cold, lashing and horizontal. We had no choice but to cross a huge boulder field and the rain turned the rocks' smooth surfaces into glass. They were a nightmare to traverse, with constant slips and falls, and I wondered in these moments if life as a civilian would really be so bad! That patrol was harder than many of the marches I'd done on selection and not something that I'll ever forget.

We did what we needed to do, however, and got where we needed to go. Myself and Scobie then set up as rear protection, while the other pair in the patrol went on a little further, where they could get eyes on the house.

Due to the conditions, Scobie was on the verge of hypothermia. Isolated as we were, it was a situation that could turn deadly very quickly and I got plenty of hot brews into him and kept him as dry as possible under my shelter sheet. Scobie recovered quickly and thanked me.

'No problem, mate. That's what medics are for.'

We weren't in the best of moods after the boulder field and when it became obvious that the house was empty, I wondered why we'd embarked on such a pointless mission. As night approached, we marked and waited at the Helicopter Landing

Site (HLS) as planned, but when the Wessex came in and we clambered aboard, we were given three days' worth of rations to put in our kit – instead of going back to the *Sir Lancelot*, we were going straight onto another patrol.

The Wessex flew us to another location on the West Island and we were briefed to expect a landing of Argentinian paratroopers at any time. Our task was to overlook the potential drop zone (DZ) and if an enemy C-130 appeared, we were to shoot it out of the sky. This would obviously cause a massive loss of life, but war is war. None of us had any hesitation about the orders: if anything, we all wanted to be the one to fire the Stinger. We certainly weren't squeamish about such things.

We laid up for a couple of days overlooking the suspected drop zone, but the enemy didn't show. Disappointed, cold and wet, we were taken back to the *Sir Lancelot*.

It was there that we were given grave news. Our patrols hadn't been the only ones on the ground. The regiment had sent two men into Port Howard on an intelligence gathering mission. They'd been compromised, had come under fire and Captain John Hamilton had been killed. His signaller, Roy Fonseka, was captured. Unfortunately for him, his equipment included kit taken from the enemy and this greatly angered the Argentinian forces – I imagine they thought he'd taken it from their dead comrades, which he may well have done, to be quite honest. That was where I'd gotten my parka, after all.

The enemy interrogators were hostile to say the least and threatened to shoot Roy, but he gave nothing away except his name, rank and number. The local commander had enough and sent a message to his superior in Stanley, making him aware that he planned to execute Roy. Thankfully, the commander could see that the writing was on the wall and that they were going to lose the war – he told his subordinate to keep Roy alive and this made good sense. I expect he thought that they could expect no quarter from us if they gave none themselves. The British fleet intercepted these messages and, knowing Roy was safe for now, decided that launching a hostage rescue mission would do more harm than good. Roy would be on his own until the war ended, but we all knew that he could hack it – he was a tough cookie.

One interesting thing to come out of this engagement was that the enemy were so impressed by Captain Hamilton's courage that they recommended to the British that he receive an award. For giving Roy covering fire and a chance to escape, Captain Hamilton was posthumously awarded the Military Cross – he was a true hero of the regiment.

* * *

I can't say that I was particularly comfortable on the *Sir Lancelot*. We ate well and were able to take showers and wash the grime off us, so no complaints there. We also had space and the crew were friendly, but I couldn't help thinking what had happened to *Lancelot*'s sister ship only days before.

The *Sir Galahad* had been at anchor at Port Pleasant to unload the Welsh Guards when it was attacked by A4 Skyhawks and hit by at least two bombs. Fires began to burn uncontrollably and many men died in the bowels of the ship. A Chinese crewman, Chiu Yiu-Nam, was later awarded the George Medal for saving at least 10 men, but unfortunately, 48 others died on the *Sir Galahad*, with 32 of them from the Welsh Guards.

I'm aware that there may be the benefit of hindsight in my opinion here, but it seemed to us at the time – and still does now – that the *Sir Galahad* was an accident waiting to happen. Or more accurately, perhaps, a sitting duck waiting to be killed. Despite suffering losses in the campaign, a lot of things were breaking our way and I think that can breed a certain kind of arrogance – if it doesn't exist in decision makers already. Casualties are inevitable in war, but that doesn't mean that *all* casualties are and I think that the *Sir Galahad* was one such example.

And the losses on 8 June didn't stop there. A landing craft from *Fearless* was sunk and several other ships were damaged. After the losses in San Carlos Water, I made sure I was always accommodated in the upper decks and I was much happier being cold on land than warm on a ship. The thought of being trapped in a vessel that was ablaze was absolutely terrifying – give me enemy small arms any day of the week!

But, as they say, you should be careful what you wish for!

11

TROOP ATTACK

As 'The Big Push' gathered momentum on East Falkland, we prepared for our own part in the assaults. With the entirety of what was left of the squadron we redeployed to Mount Kent and from there patrolled to Beagle Ridge, a small ridge running east from Mount Harriet, which 42 Commando would clear in the days to come. Beagle wasn't very high and we stood off from it and watched for a while. There were enemy present and they made little effort to hide that fact – their poor camouflage and concealment, and sloppy routine told me that these were not top-rate troops.

Still, you don't need to be the best to get lucky, particularly if you hold the high ground. We estimated the enemy number to be about 30 and the officer commanding (OC) decided that Air Troop would put in an attack:

Hey, diddle diddle, straight up the middle! Sounds good to me, boss!

When I was an infantry soldier, we were told that attacking troops should always try and outnumber the enemy three to one. For our attack, *they* would outnumber *us*, two to one.

I can't say that bothered myself or the other lads: we believed in ourselves and our training. We would conduct the assault in daylight, with Nick and PJ providing fire support from the General Purpose Machine Gun (GPMG), a 7.26mm belt-fed machine gun in its Sustained Fire (SF) role – this meant that the gun would be mounted on a large tripod, enabling it to give accurate fire in long bursts. In the light role, the GPMG gunner usually fires bursts of three to five rounds, but in the SF role, would be squeezing off long bursts of up to 20. This would keep the enemy's head down so that the rest of us could get close with small arms, grenades and, if needed, bayonets.

In front of the enemy's defensive positions was a huge lone rock. You'd almost think there wasn't a war on as this rock seemed to be the place for the enemy to hang out and chat. Once they spotted us, however, they soon ran back to their fighting positions!

I was excited about the upcoming action and in no doubt that we would be successful. That didn't mean that I thought it would be easy. Against superior numbers and attacking in daylight, I reckoned that we would take some casualties, but not for one moment did I entertain the idea that I'd be wounded myself, let alone killed. I was going home at the end of this war and that was that – I wonder if the enemy thought the same?

Not everyone was quite as certain as me, though, and one of our troop looked like he was having second thoughts about his chosen profession! He seemed a little nervous – or 'windy' as my dad's generation would say. So I did what any good mate would do to help him and whispered soothing words in his ear about how everything would be OK.

Only joking! I smacked him hard across the face.

This did the trick and focused his mind on something other than 'what ifs'. He soon calmed down and I hoped he'd remain that way. He was carrying a GPMG in the light role, meaning the gun was carried in hand and not mounted on a tripod as it is in the SF role. We needed him. Well, more accurately, we needed the gun that he carried. That weapon system is a battle winner because of the amount of fire it can provide. So good, in fact, that the British Army is still using it 40 years after the Falklands – some things can't be improved upon!

We needed our gunner in the fight and there was no time for niceties in that moment. I'd have hit him again if I needed to. Sometimes actions speak louder than words.

The GPMG in the SF role was supposed to be firing long bursts onto the enemy position to keep their heads down as we attacked, but a series of pathetic single shots was all that would come from it – not good! Regardless, the boss gave the signal to advance and we moved forward towards the enemy trenches. While keeping my eyes ahead for the enemy, I moved from one piece of cover to the next. Perhaps I moved too quickly because the next time I looked around I was on my own!

Luckily for me, the only ones moving faster than me were the enemy. At the first sight of our attack, they jumped out of their trenches and legged it! So I arrived at their fighting positions alone. Looking back down the slope, I saw that the rest of my troop had stopped. What the hell was wrong with them? It was then that I looked around me and realised that I had run straight through a minefield! Silly bastard. Thankfully, I found a goat track and followed this back down to the rest of the troop.

I asked why the GPMG SF had only been firing single shots. It turned out that PJ had stripped the barrel for cleaning, but replaced the gas plug the wrong way! It was stoppage after stoppage until Nick figured out the issue and swapped the barrels, but by then I was already at the trenches.

The enemy positions were a mess. There was rubbish and kit everywhere and it was obvious from this that they were a platoon of ill-disciplined conscripts – no wonder they'd run in the face of the professionals (backwards gas plugs notwithstanding). We'd later discover that some of these conscripts had less than 10 days' training before being sent to war. If you ask me, their real enemy wasn't us, but the people who sent them – they didn't stand a chance against British forces.

It transpired that some Argentinian officers would shoot their men if they tried to run, but that didn't seem to be an issue for this platoon. They'd all scarpered. We'd taken Beagle Ridge with no casualties and barely needed to clean our weapons.

We remained in the captured positions as 42 Commando put in their assault on the more stoutly defended Mount

Harriet. It was part of the brigade push and we watched as the night sky filled with tracer fire and the flash of explosions. From a distance it all looked very pretty, but on the slopes, men were fighting and killing each other in the most gruesome of ways.

* * *

On the night of 11 June, as well as the attack on Mount Harriet, the infantry force also launched attacks on Mount Longdon and Two Sisters. The capture of these heights was vital to secure the approach to Port Stanley. The mountains around the town needed to be taken so that the infantry could advance on the enemy at sea level and liberate the settlement. In war, be it a building or a mountain, height is essential. If the mountains were in enemy hands, they would be able to pour fire down on us on the flatter areas around Port Stanley, not to mention launch raids or even full-scale attacks into our rear and flanks. In the Pacific campaign of the Second World War, the US Marines had taken one island after another to advance on Japan, a process known as 'island hopping'. The push on Port Stanley was similar to this, except that instead of hopping from island to island, our infantry would be fighting a succession of battles from mountain to mountain. At the end of these, Port Stanley awaited. Nobody knew if the enemy would make a stand there, or if they would surrender once the dominating high ground was taken. At that point, when we held the high ground as well as the sea, surely they would realise the jig was up? But that's putting the cart before the horse. The enemy weren't about to surrender just to make us happy and so assaults on the mountains would have to be made.

42 Commando would be the main force for the assault on Harriet, supported by engineers, artillery and a reserve of Welsh Guards, no doubt eager to get stuck into the enemy after suffering the horrors of the *Sir Galahad*.

A naval bombardment was put in, the side of the mountain seeming to be covered with flame as the shells burst. Flares were fired into the sky, casting the battlefields into eerie shades of red and yellow. Tracer fire arced all over the slopes and sky.

K Company began their advance undetected and used their Commando daggers to silence two enemy sentries. The battle began to break up into a series of melees and actions between smaller units, rock formations, pockets of darkness and trenches all needing to be cleared of enemy. There were also minefields on the slopes and these didn't distinguish between enemy and friendly feet, causing casualties in both forces.

Argentinian soldiers – mostly conscripts – began throwing up their hands to surrender, but other groups put up a stiff resistance. As they had done at Goose Green, British MILAN anti-tank missiles proved excellent ways of knocking out enemy strong points. Unlike Goose Green, however, this battle had started and ended in darkness and before the sun had come up, 42 Commando had secured all of their objectives, paying the solemn price of two men killed and 30 wounded.

Despite this apparent success, 42 had actually come up short of their mission's goals as they had expected to also take Mount William in the same night. Stubborn pockets of enemy resistance had scuppered that plan and perhaps, as at Goose Green, our planning officers had underestimated the enemy and the difficulties of traversing battlefields at night – particularly those sewn with minefields.

There was also the discovery that the Argentinians were better equipped than the British infantry and not just in cold weather gear, but in night sights: bought from America, of course! Training was their undoing. Not only were they not trained to the same standard as our men individually, but their commanders had made very basic errors: by not extending their positions from one end of the mountain to the other, they had left themselves open to being rolled up on a flank. More than 300 of them were taken prisoner by our Commandos, a job well done.

* * *

As 42 Commando were doing battle on Mount Harriet, 3 Para were assaulting the slopes of Mount Longdon. Again, darkness and the chaos of fighting in rock formations made hard work of keeping order and enemy troops that had been missed would appear in the rear of flanks of the advancing

Paras. For three hours, violent hand-to-hand combat raged on the mountainside, the Paras putting their bayonets to use to clear out enemy positions. The enemy sent reinforcements and their rifles' night sights proved deadly, hitting many British soldiers. The attacking Paras were met by storms of fire. Sergeant McKay disregarded his own safety and charged the enemy positions alone, lobbing grenades into their positions until he was killed – for his actions, he would be awarded the Victoria Cross posthumously.

With so many wounded, the Paras had to withdraw from some of the ground so that they could consolidate, including protection of their casualties. While the wounded were recovered, the dead had to be left where they'd fallen and several of them had their maroon berets taken from them by Argentinian soldiers as spoils of war.

Perhaps the British forces and commanders had underestimated their enemy once again. The Paras pulled back far enough so that 29 Commando's guns on Mount Kent could smash the peaks with 105mm shellfire and then 3 Para went back into the attack.

Through dogged determination and an unwillingness to lose, the paratroopers beat back the Argentinian counterattacks and eventually secured Mount Longdon. Eighteen British soldiers died, including two who were just 17 years old. A further five servicemen would die in the further two days of shelling that the Argentinians would put onto the slopes.

Altogether, there would be more than 50 British wounded on Longdon and 31 enemy dead, with 120 wounded and 50 taken prisoner. A hard night and one full of bravery on both sides.

* * *

The assaulting force for Two Sisters was primarily made up of 45 Commando and they initially made very quick gains along the high ground with no resistance. Then, at about 2300 hours, they came under sustained and accurate fire, and for several hours, X Company were held up on the side of the mountain. Using naval gunfire to hit the enemy positions, 45's CO realised that one of his companies would not be enough to get the job done and brought up two more from his reserve.

Y and Z Companies fought a two-hour battle to drive the enemy from the northern peak. There was brave resistance from the Argentinian defenders, some of whom fought a rear-guard action to allow their comrades to escape towards Port Stanley. Others took up blocking positions between Mount Tumbledown and Wireless Ridge, where more battles would soon have to be fought. Like the Paras on Mount Longdon, the Bootnecks on Two Sisters came under artillery fire once they had pushed the enemy out of their positions, causing several casualties – some of them from hearing loss after surviving near misses. On 13 June, A4 Skyhawks put in an attack, result-ing in severe damage to three Gazelle helicopters.

All in all, however, the battle was a complete success. Seven Royal Marines and one Commando Sapper died in the assault, as well as 20 of the enemy. And there was, unfortunately, further tragedy when HMS *Glamorgan* – which had been supporting the attack – was hit by a land-based Exocet missile, killing 14 of her crew. Given the strength of the enemy defensive positions on the mountain, it could have been a lot worse.

The night of 11 June, in particular, was a bloody one for the task force, but none of us had come here expecting that it would be any other way. Casualties had been taken and given, but the objectives had been carried out and the end of the war was a big step closer.

* * *

While those battles were taking place, up on our ridge we watched through our NVGs as enemy C130s flew into Stanley airport, ferrying men and supplies. Seven raids had been carried out by RAF Vulcan bombers against this target, but none had been able to damage the runway to the point where it was inoperable. To this day, I don't know why the navy didn't sail into this area to deny the airport through naval gunfire. Perhaps it was due to the threat of land-based Exocets, I just don't know. Besides, it didn't look like the enemy would be able to hold onto the airfield for much longer as our grip was tightening around the town and the mountains overlooking it.

On the night of 13 June, the task force launched an assault on Mount Tumbledown, the action primarily carried out by the Scots Guards. Not only were the enemy well dug in on these slopes, but they were also using Tumbledown to direct deadly artillery fire onto Mount Longdon, which had recently been seized by 3 Para. A smaller, diversionary attack would begin the battle before the main force advanced silently for as long as possible.

Two British soldiers were killed when the enemy opened fire. After two hours of fighting, the enemy began to withdraw before the diversionary attack and the Guards secured their abandoned positions. The Argentinians then showed signs of launching a counterattack and, not wanting to get cut off, the men of the diversionary attack began to withdraw. Unfortunately, they suffered several casualties in a minefield and the enemy heaped on the misery with mortar fire.

Those casualties were not in vain as the diversion allowed the rest of the battalion to reach their objective undetected. As had been the case on other mounts, the enemy had not extended their positions fully along the high ground. For several hours, Argentinian Marines and infantry mixed it up with the British assaulting force. The two sides were so close that they could exchange insults as well as bullets, and as the battle dragged on into the night, a decision was looming: pull back and try again the next night, or keep going and risk being out on the slopes when it got light and even the enemy without night vision would be able to pick off their targets.

It was the tenacity of the Scots Guards that proved the deciding factor. Major Kiszely led from the front, breaking his bayonet in half as he killed an enemy soldier. This action inspired his men, who were soon getting to work with bayonets themselves. Once they had a moment to catch their breath, the men realised that they could see Port Stanley beneath them. Kiszely was awarded the Military Cross and the Scots Guards were awarded a victory. Supporting actions, including one fought by the Welsh Guards, were also successful. By 0900, the objectives were secure, paid for with the lives of nine British soldiers and 35 wounded. The enemy dead were three times the number, with several of them killed by British bayonets.

* * *

One of the final obstacles in the way of liberating Port Stanley was Wireless Ridge, an area of high ground with dominating views onto the settlement and the low ground that would need to be used to approach it. If Wireless Ridge could be wrestled from the enemy, the end of the war could be only days away. And so, on the night of 13 June, two weeks removed from their hard battle at Goose Green, 2 Para were tasked with taking it.

Lieutenant Colonel 'H' Jones's replacement, Lieutenant Colonel David Chaundler, had parachuted into the sea before taking command of 2 Para. One of his first points of action was to emphasise that 2 Para would not go into any other battle without fire support, as they had done at Goose Green. So, on Wireless Ridge, 2 Para would be supported by naval gunfire and the 105mm guns of 29 Commando, as well as a troop of Scimitar light armoured vehicles from the Blues & Royals, which are armed with 30mm cannon that fire high-explosive rounds.

Wireless Ridge received an absolute pasting before the Paras advanced: so much so that when D Company reached their objectives on the hill, the enemy had already scarpered. A and B Company were not so lucky and came across stiff resistance on their objectives. However, they soon won the fire-fight with the use of their own machine guns and artillery and pushed the enemy out. The enemy also had airborne soldiers on Wireless Ridge and so it was paratrooper vs paratrooper.

The maroon-wearing British won the fight.

As we would later find out, towards the end of the battle, the Argentinian commander in the fight had been offered the use of Skyhawks armed with napalm to attack the British force. The commander had declined, apparently worried what the British would do in retaliation – he sounds like a smart cookie. Not that I would ever suggest 2 Para would break the rules of engagement, but surrender becomes a bit more diffi-cult when you drop burning fuel on top of people and men have been forced to listen to the screams of their dying friends as they're burnt alive. Besides, judging by the Skyhawk attack at Goose Green, the commander may have been worried that they'd dump it on his own men.

It made no difference in the end. Wireless Ridge was taken, another domino fallen. British casualties were 14, including three dead. Twenty-five of the enemy were killed and five times that number wounded.

It was another bloody night, but the mountains had been cleared and Port Stanley waited below them. The end wasn't only in sight, but within touching distance. However, before that could happen, and while all this was going on, the men of D Squadron were given our own chance to die for Queen and country.

12

THE FINAL DAY

Up until now D Squadron's operations in the Falklands had felt fairly low-level. Quite often the targets we were sent out to recce turned out to be nothing and the one deliberate attack we had conducted was easier going than the ranges in Sennybridge Training Area – well, except for the minefield! That wasn't the case for everyone, of course. The Guards, Paras and Commandos had all had a time of it, but they had cleared out the enemy wherever they found them. Much of the enemy had run away to join their comrades dug in and around Port Stanley.

I expected that the Argentinians would put up a fight in the town. I could understand why conscripts would run, but surely, now that they were alongside regular Marine units and not fighting on the mountains, they would put up a firm fight in their final chance to halt the tide of British victories? I wanted to be involved in that battle when it happened, but first, we had another job to do.

Our target was an oil refinery outside of Port Stanley. It was on a small inlet and the intelligence corps promised that it was lightly defended. Hmmm… I wasn't buying that one for a second, but ours not to reason why!

D and G Squadron's mission was to go in and destroy the refinery oil tanks and to me, this seemed bonkers for a couple of reasons. First, if we wanted to blow up the tanks, why not send in a Harrier to do so? And second, why were we destroying infrastructure when the war was clearly going to be over soon? It made no sense to me at all, but the task force commanders weren't asking me for my opinion.

The plan to accomplish the mission was simple: using the small sized and largely unprotected Rigid Raider assault craft, Boat Troop would cross the sound under cover of darkness to destroy the oil tanks. G Squadron and the rest of D would be further up the inlet and we'd provide fire support from small arms and anti-tank MILAN missiles, which are fired from a man-portable launcher. After the initial reservations about why we were doing this, I started to feel excited. It had felt like we were on the sidelines when the infantry battalions put their attacks in on the mountains and I wanted another chance to get in on the action. I think the other lads felt the same as after a bit of grumbling, we were getting into the spirit and up for a scrap.

Looking back, we must have been spotted from the moment we left Beagle Ridge to head to our forming-up point. Artillery shells began to whine through the air and explode in the sky – they'd been set on variable timers so that the shrapnel would rain downwards, rather than allow the boggy ground to soak up much of the explosion. Fortunately for us, the rounds never quite got above our position, but it was bloody unpleasant to say the least and I wondered what it must have been like for my father in his Lancaster, surrounded by the bangs of exploding flak during the Second World War.

Mercifully, we arrived at our fire support positions behind a bank of peat and waited for H-Hour – the moment when we would open fire and Boat Troop would begin their assault from the landing area.

Boat Troop hadn't been on the end of the shells like we had and, believing they were still undetected, they got into their Rigid Raiders and crossed the choppy waters of the sound towards the refinery. As they hit the shore, the world erupted into gunfire.

The enemy opened up with such a heavy rate of fire that Boat Troop didn't even make it off the beach. What was supposed to be a sneak attack was met with a ferocious and withering defence, and any expectations that this mission would be a doddle went out of the window. They needed our help. Air Troop rose up from behind the cover of the peat embankment to give support, but before we could even begin to shoot, we came on the end of the most accurate fire I have ever experienced in my life. There were so many bullets and cannon shells in the air that I could feel them displacing the air above my head, a storm of steel that I begrudgingly respected, one professional soldier to another.

Under such an assault I had no choice but to face down into the peat, the musty smell filling my nostrils. With PJ, I tried to get the GPMG SF into action, but any sign of movement over the lip was met with a heavy hail of fire. The enemy had an observation team on the high ground and they were directing small arms and anti-aircraft cannon fire right onto us – the little lip of peat was all that was keeping us alive.

PJ and I looked at each other and laughed. When you're pinned down and full of adrenaline, what else can you do but see the funny side? Boat Troop needed our help, but it was certain death to raise our heads – so much for the light resistance that the intelligence corps had promised us!

Out of sight to us, Boat Troop beat a retreat to their landing craft, the water around them churned up by the enemy fire. They got on board but not without taking casualties. The landing craft offered no protection from the fire, and if not for the quick thinking of some members of the troop, there's a good chance they'd have all been killed.

Sitting in the sound was an Argentinian hospital ship and Boat Troop raced towards it, putting the ship between themselves and the enemy. The Argentinians had to check their fire, but already there was blood in the rigid raider's hulls. It was time for us to pull back. I didn't know how we'd be able to do that under such intense and accurate fire, and so I started to prepare myself for the possibility that we'd have to spend all day face down in the mud before withdrawing under cover of darkness. And then…

Silence.

What had been a storm above our heads was now calm. I can't explain why the enemy were willing to let us leave, but we didn't wait around to find out – we legged it! It wasn't the most glorious moment of our careers, but sometimes survival comes first. We were on the edge of the enemy's range and we didn't have to go too far until we felt like we could relax and share a laugh. Some of the lads sparked up cigarettes and we all had a similar look on our faces. One that said, 'that was a bit hairy!' Ah well, whatever doesn't kill you makes you stronger.

We met Boat Troop back at the squadron RV. After the amount of fire they'd taken I expected a large number of casualties and so I was massively relieved to find out that only two of their number had got hit and neither of them was critical. It felt like a miracle. D Squadron had walked into the jaws of death but somehow we had come out with everyone alive – luck was certainly on our side that night.

A Gazelle helicopter was sent to CASVAC (casualty evacuation) the two wounded and the boss told me to go with them as a medic. Wanting to encourage the lads, I patted one of them on the leg.

'Stop that,' he said, 'that's where I'm hit.'

Oops!

The aid station was set up at the back of Estancia House. Thankfully, there was little work for the doctors and nurses that night and they soon saw to the lads. Confident they were in the best of hands, I went outside to look for a place to set up my basha, which is the shelter that a soldier builds himself in the field, usually by using a ground sheet or poncho. Someone from the house must have spotted me building my humble abode and a kindly woman opened the door to the house:

'Come in here,' she said, 'you can sleep in the living room.'

We spoke a little more but I don't really remember much of it. After the adrenaline of the day, and having come in from the cold I was knackered, but what luxury! Not long ago I'd been face down in the peat, bullets cracking over my head, and now here I was in front of the fire with a hot cup of tea – life can change very quickly. It was then that I made a huge mistake and took off my boots. I'd done the same on the infamous NCO cadre from hell, back in 1976. Back then, I'd put my feet in front of a coal fire and gotten very painful frost nip as the circulation came back too quickly. The same happened here in Estancia House and I was suddenly in a lot of pain. But every cloud has a silver lining and the pain brought back nice memories of a warm fire at home!

Thinking of Jenny, I drifted off to sleep. By the time that I woke up, the war was over.

13

THE BUTCHER'S BILL

Tho' much is taken, much abides;

And tho' we are not now

That strength which in old days

Moved earth and heaven,

That which we are, we are;

One equal temper of heroic hearts,

Made weak by time and fate,

But strong in will,

To strive, to seek, to find,

And not to yield.

Ulysses (excerpt) by Alfred Tennyson, 1842

The morning after the attack on the oil refinery, word spread that a conditional ceasefire had been accepted by the commanders of the enemy forces present on the islands. I had mixed feelings about it, to be quite honest. The night before we had been beaten back by the enemy and like any professional soldier, I didn't want to end the campaign on the back foot. On the other hand, I knew that we were very lucky to have come out of last night's fight without losing any more of the squadron. The attack on the refinery could well have cost us several lives and so a part of me was happy to know that we wouldn't be losing any more of the men – D Squadron had paid a high price already.

When the plan to attack the refinery had been hatched, I didn't understand why we were attacking it at all, so close to the end of the campaign. And if it was that important, I didn't understand why Harriers couldn't be sent to do the job. I was pissed off to say the least when we then discovered that the ceasefire had been signed before we set off on the mission! We almost lost men in a war that was already won. I was livid with our commanders for that – what was the point?

The surrender that General Menendez made to Brigadier Moore was that his officers would be permitted to retain their firearms – I expect this was to protect them from their own men, some of whom would no doubt want revenge for the way they were treated by their commanders. It would later emerge that the enlisted men were beaten, tortured, thrown into mock graves and subjected to mock executions by their officers – no wonder many of them were so quick to surrender to British forces.

Argentina had gone to war to distract from their failing economy and failures of the country's leadership. Well, if the Junta wanted a distraction, they'd got it. Like every bill in war, the cost was men and materials. The enemy paid a heavy price. And when I say 'the enemy', I am of course referring to the young men that the Junta sent to fight and die on their behalf. Not one of the country's leadership was anywhere near the warzone. Instead, the force they sent had a large number of conscripts who had less than 10 days' training. As I've said, a British soldier's *basic* training is 10 weeks, so they were sending them out to fail and potentially lose their lives. The enemy's leadership made me sick and still does – cowards to a man. By contrast, many of their men showed bravery and honour. Their Butcher's Bill (a term referring to loss of life dating back to Napoleonic times) was as follows:

Total enemy dead: 649*
Total enemy wounded: 1,188
Total enemy captured: 11,313
Enemy aircraft lost: 89 (45 destroyed in the air,
20 destroyed on the ground, 27 captured, one lost with
the *Belgrano*, six lost in accidents).

To say it was a disaster for the enemy was an understatement. Argentina had around 240 military aircraft in service at the beginning of the war. Six weeks later, they'd lost almost half of

---

* 'Ley 24.950: Decláranse "Héroes nacionales" a los combatientes argentinos fallecidos durante la guerra de Malvinas'. InfoLEG (in Spanish). 18 March 1998. Retrieved 11 March 2015.

them. Of course, aircraft can be replaced. Not so the men who flew them. Some of the bravest acts of the campaign involved the enemy pilots flying into thick anti-aircraft fire. They knew their only chance to win the war was to keep us from landing and despite their losses, they came again and again. As one warrior to another, I salute them.

If there was a silver lining for the country of Argentina in this loss, it was that the disastrous campaign was a nail in the coffin of the military Junta, who were already responsible for many crimes against their people. In 1983 they were replaced with a democratic government and the country began to heal. The anniversary of the criminal dictatorship's rise to power, on 24 March, is remembered in Argentina as the Day of Remembrance for Truth and Justice. I am proud to have played a small part in the downfall of a regime that killed 30,000 of its own people, but any feelings like this come with the benefit of hindsight – at the time I was just incredibly angry. They had invaded British lands. We had come to clear them out. In doing so, we had lost hundreds of men, including 22 of our brothers on the Sea King crash. Those men had died for the enemy to just throw his hands up when we were in sight of Port Stanley? Their cowardice sickened me. It was so unfair that they could cause this war then just decide that they'd had enough and throw up their hands. They would be going home, my mates wouldn't.

I was fucking furious. I still am to this day and for good reason. According to a report issued by the Ministry of Defence in 2013,* the deaths of British personnel and citizens in the campaign were as follows:

Royal Navy: 87

British Army: 123

Royal Air Force: 1

Royal Fleet Auxiliary: 4

Merchant Navy: 6

Hong Chinese sailors: 8

Falkland Islanders: 3

Of course, the deaths from war do not stop when the last bullet has been fired. At the time of the report, 247 Falklands War veterans had died of 'external causes', made up primarily of suicides and open verdict deaths. That's not to say that these suicides were the result of war – or war alone – but given what we now know about PTSD (post-traumatic stress disorder) and moral injury, I think it's fair to say that the war followed many a man home and proved fatal in the end.

In terms of material, Britain's maritime forces lost:

HMS *Sheffield*

HMS *Ardent*

HMS *Antelope*

---

* https://assets.publishing.service.gov.uk/government/uploads/system/uploads/attachment_data/file/365217/Falkland-deaths-31_december_2012.pdf

HMS *Coventry*

SS *Atlantic Conveyor*

RFA *Sir Galahad*

Landing Craft Unit H4, from HMS *Fearless*.

Several other ships were damaged, including some that required towing back to the UK for repair. Britain's air losses were:

Fixed wing

Sea Harrier: 6

Harrier GR3: 4

Total: 10

Helicopter

Sea King: 5

Wessex: 9

Lynx: 3

Gazelle: 3

Scout: 2

Chinook: 3

Total: 25*

On top of the deaths and material losses were hundreds of wounded and credit must go to the medical staff of the task force who cared for them, saving lives in adverse conditions.

---

* *Air War South Atlantic* , Jeffrey Ethell and Alfred Price, Macmillan, 1983.

Nowadays it is common practice to repatriate British war dead for burial in their home towns, but in 1982 the practice was to bury the fallen close to the battlegrounds on which they died. The British dead were buried at Blue Beach Cemetery, close to where the landings had been made. Later, a memorial would be built at the site, with the following words engraved beside the names of the men remembered there:

1982

APRIL–JUNE

IN HONOUR OF

THE SOUTH ATLANTIC TASK FORCE

AND TO THE ABIDING MEMORY OF

THE SAILORS, SOLDIERS AND AIRMEN

WHO GAVE THEIR LIVES AND WHO

HAVE NO GRAVE BUT THE SEA

HERE BESIDE THE

GRAVES OF THEIR COMRADES THIS

MEMORIAL RECORDS THEIR NAMES

GIVE GLORY TO THE LORD AND

DECLARE HIS PRAISE IN THE ISLANDS

In 1984, a family of one of the fallen would request that the Ministry of Defence (MOD) repatriate their loved one to the UK so that he could be buried close to home. In light of this, an offer was made to all families of the Falklands War dead to bring their boys home. Sixty-four families asked for this to happen and the men were brought home on the RFA *Sir Bedivere* in the winter of 1984.

Of course, it wasn't possible to bring everyone home, or even make the offer. One hundred and seventy-four of the dead were buried at sea or lost with their aircraft and their bodies were not recovered. The sunken ships and crash sites remain Commonwealth war graves and of course that includes the Sea King aboard which the SAS lost 22 of their best.

We will remember them.

14

HOMECOMING

On 15 June, with the war over, and myself at the aid station, I needed to find my way back to the squadron. I didn't know exactly where they were and so I hitched a lift to Port Stanley, confident that I could then link up with them wherever they were.

Flying into the football field that was acting as the Gazelle flight line, I got my first real look at Port Stanley, the capital of the Falkland Islands. A town of less than 2,000 people, it was a tiny place, its brightly painted rooftops a splash of colour against the bleak landscape of moorland and ridgelines. Old whaling ships rusted in the harbour and from the air, I could see the congregations of enemy prisoners.

It was a strange thing seeing the enemy, and so many of them. The Paras were providing the guard force and it seemed no matter where you looked, there were enemy weapons dumped in piles and large groups of the enemy huddled together under guard.

I had a mate over at the Gazelle squadron – Johno, who I had first met on exercise in Kenya. With a few other blokes we took a look at the kit and equipment that the enemy had left behind. I was window shopping for a souvenir if I saw something that took my fancy, but I was also just drawn to the piles of weapons that had been meant to kill us now lying discarded in piles – it was such a strange sight. Most of the weapons were rifles and I didn't think Jenny would be too happy with me turning up with something as big as that. As a soldier it is unusual to see a weapon unattended, let alone piles of them left to rust in the rain, and I feel sorry for any OCD sergeant major who had to witness this horror of war. After taking a look, I joined the Air Corps lads for a brew in their operations room, which had been set up in the changing rooms of the football pitch.

I didn't have anything on me to trade, but one of the lads handed me an enemy Colt 45, a famous model of pistol that first entered use in 1911. The reason the pistol was still in service was because it was so good at its job and I was delighted to have such an incredible souvenir to take home with me – it was just the right size to keep in a lock box at home.

I wanted to take a walk around Port Stanley and see more of the place and the people that we had been fighting for, but a ride had been arranged to reunite me with the rest of the squadron, who were back aboard the *Sir Lancelot*. A Gazelle helicopter dropped me off on her flight deck and the mood was jubilant to say the least – everyone knew they were going home alive and would be doing so victorious. It was a party, but

I couldn't get in the mood. I felt cheated. Like the enemy had promised us something, then backed out after we had already paid the price. I was disgusted by their cowardice. Sickened at the waste of life.

All this way and all those men, for this?

Even if I wasn't in agony with my feet, I would have been in no mood to party. I found my bed space, took my boots off and the pain was instantaneous. After I pulled off my socks, I saw that my feet were white, swollen and wrinkled. I knew at once I had trench foot – something else to thank the fucking enemy for.

Taking off my boots had been like flicking a switch and from that point on, I couldn't put weight on my feet for weeks. The lads had to bring me my meals and I crawled to the toilets on my hands and knees. Where I had been angry, now I was miserable and *fucking angry*.

With the help of the lads I attended the taking of the official squadron photograph – I wasn't going to miss out on that, pain be damned! We looked like a bunch of pirates, many of us with droopy moustaches, shaggy hair and a mixture of British Army, Royal Navy and captured enemy clothing.

We were the men who had 'beaten the clock'.

And we weren't leaving empty-handed. I had my Colt 45 and the lads were taking their own souvenirs: rifles and helmets were popular. I couldn't go with them because of my feet – which just put me in a worse mood – but the other lads caught helicopter rides into Port Stanley so that they could meet the people they had come to fight for, take a look at the enemy and find some more souvenirs to take home.

When General Menéndez had invaded the islands, General Galtieri, the head of Argentina's Junta, had presented him with a large statue made of bronze – quite a piece and I must say that it looks lovely in the officers' mess at Hereford! How did it get there? Well, you may find a clue in a photograph of the CO's signaller leaving the Governor's house with a very large and very heavy-looking bergen: to the victor the spoils. If that award was given for taking the islands, then we were surely the rightful owners.

I didn't get to see Port Stanley again after I'd returned to the *Sir Lancelot*, so all of my news came from the other lads. Apparently, welfare of the prisoners of war was an issue. This wasn't because they were being mistreated by the British prisoner handlers, but they were living in the open (no different to what we'd had to do to win the war). Feeding them was not an issue and the prisoners were given shipping containers full of ration packs to distribute, but repatriating them to Argentinian soil was a priority. No matter how angry I was, none of us wanted the enemy prisoners to die due to exposure. With constant rain and low temperatures, a speedy solution to this problem really was a matter of life and death.

The issue was that the Argentinian Junta had not formally ended the war, even though the local commanders had surrendered. If we gave the enemy back their men, they could be attacking us again in the very same war. I think it speaks highly of the British spirit and sense of justice that we did this anyway. We would rather risk a double-cross than be the ones responsible for possibly hundreds of deaths from hypothermia, and with the help of the 'Governor' that Argentina had installed on the islands, a repatriation was organised with speed.

On 18 June 1982, 10,000 Argentinian servicemen were taken from the Falklands on board the SS *Canberra* and the SS *Norland* and repatriated to the Argentinian mainland. Approximately 1,000 prisoners of war were held back on the islands. Mostly officers, they would remain until the Junta formally accepted terms a short time later.

We later learned that a phone line had been opened between the Argentinian staff officers in Port Stanley and British HQ in San Carlos. This development was the initiative of Colonel Rose of our regiment and an islander. The line proved very important and I believe it helped shorten the suffering of the enemy and prevented damage to Port Stanley, as it helped convince the Argentinians that their cause was lost and that surrender was the only option.

After a week or so on the ship we received news that Princess Diana had given birth to an heir: welcome to the world, Prince William! It was another moment to feed the patriotism that was in the air and I imagine this must have been how it felt to be alive in the Victorian era: military victories in a far-flung corner of the world and a tot of rum to toast royalty.

'Splicing the mainbrace', the navy call it. The crew line up to get a shot, but when D Squadron reached the front of the line we were told that it wasn't a tradition for soldiers – well, we made it one!

'God save the Queen!'

My feet began to get back to normal, with the inflammation going down and far less pain. I was very happy to get above decks and feel the elements on my face. A lot of vessels were at anchor and helicopters were buzzing back and forth between them.

Looking back at the islands, I could see the mountains and ridgelines that men had fought and died for. Seeing the harsh conditions and knowing what it had taken to win the islands back, I could take some pride in knowing that I had played my part and that D Squadron had answered the call on several occasions. When I joined the regiment and was badged, the regimental sergeant major (RSM) had said: 'Be there when the bell rings.' Well, we had certainly done that and I knew that I was far from done with the army: I'd been given a war, but I was still hungry for more.

* * *

The battles over, our thoughts turned to home. Though I was always certain that I'd come through alive, I'd mostly blocked out thoughts of what would come next in life. Not because I found it upsetting, or anything like that, but simply because it was a distraction. I'll give another note to young soldiers here: save making plans for home until the job is done. Every moment you're thinking about the future is taking you out of the present and in war, a split second of absent-mindedness is enough to make sure you'll never live to see any of the things you were thinking about.

I can't say that we were looking forward to sailing all the way back to the UK, but being in the special forces has its privileges. The RAF had begun landing flights at Port Stanley and my guess was that we'd be on the first flights back to Ascension and from there on to home. We were slightly pissed off (to say the least!) when it turned out that the first flights – after repatriating the wounded – would be given over to flying the press home. Weren't we the ones who'd been doing the fighting?

Still, it could have been worse. B Squadron arrived to take over from us on the *Sir Lancelot*. They were not happy and who could blame them? I might have felt cheated by a lack of resistance from the enemy, but B Squadron had gone from planned suicide mission to missing the war altogether. They must have been gutted and I had a lot of sympathy for them. Not that that stopped us from taking the piss mercilessly out of 'the war dodgers'.

We were flown from the *Lancelot* to Port Stanley airfield and boarded a C130 for Ascension. Stepping up onto the tail ramp, I left Falklands soil for the last time. I have not returned in 40 years. Perhaps one day I will, but for now, it was time to leave war behind me and return to my wife and home.

* * *

After we had landed on Ascension Island we were given a talk by the military police, who told us that it would be illegal for us to take captured weapons back to the UK. It seemed unfair and I think the army should have set up a process for us to hand in the souvenirs, get them decommissioned and then returned to us at a later date. After all, regimental messes and museums never seem short of captured weapons – why should it be different for the men who fought to take them?

One of the lads took back an FN rifle and this proved costly to him when an angry ex-wife let the police know: he got a three-year sentence for it! That seems crazy to me, but there we go.

I was annoyed about it, but I handed in the Colt 45 that I'd picked up in Port Stanley. I kept my four 105mm shell casings taken from Mount Kent and a few other bits of enemy kit, including a helmet. Years later, a co-worker of Jenny's asked if his son could borrow some of the captured kit to do a presentation at school. I was very happy to lend it and told him to keep the helmet. Unfortunately, the lovely lad died young of leukaemia some years ago and his father followed shortly after. A terrible tragedy and a reminder that we should never take life for granted, whether we are on a battlefield or in the comfort of our own homes.

I called Jenny from the ops room in Ascension and gave her the details of our incoming flight. She said she would meet me at RAF Brize Norton, as would the other troop wives. I can only imagine how relieved they must have been getting our whole troop back in one piece, minus a few breaks and flesh wounds. Jenny didn't cry, or anything like that. At least not in front of me.

I expected to find her in the arrivals area, but then I spotted her blonde hair in the airside waiting area – how the heck was she through Security? I didn't realise that she was getting the royalty treatment and we were about to get the same.

'No searching these men,' a customs officer said, 'they're the SAS!'

Bugger, I'd given up my Colt 45 for nothing!

Ah well, I soon forgot about the pistol as Jenny ran up to me and I pulled her into a hug. We kissed and I forgot what we said to each other, but there was no need for massive theatrics. I was back, she was there and that was that – all's well that ends well.

I couldn't help but notice that Jenny was the only wife who had come to Brize Norton. I don't know if that's because the other blokes had arranged to meet theirs at home, or what, but I didn't ask. I wasted no time in throwing my kit into the back of our Corolla and then we were on the road for home.

15
AFTER WAR

So what does a man do when he is born for war and the war is over? Well, first I presented Jenny with the bloodstained parka. I expected her to recoil in horror but she found it quite intriguing, especially as the ID card was still in the pocket. I kept the card, but eventually got rid of the parka. I do wonder at times what happened to the enemy soldier who was wearing it. I don't feel bad about him getting hit – he'd come to kill me and my mates – but I do wonder what he's up to. Does he have kids? What has he told them? Did he stay in the military? Is he angry that they lost? Would he do it all again? Did he grow up like me, waiting for his moment – his war?

The regiment gave us a few days off when we first got back and then we went in to sort out our weapons and equipment before going on leave for a few weeks. I suppose that we were the first troops back, other than the wounded, but there was no fanfare: we just went back to routine. As an SAS trooper you spend a lot of time away, so Jenny and I treated it like any other reunification and didn't make a fuss because it had been a war.

We booked a holiday to Greece, which was overall a lovely time. It's a strange feeling when you go from constantly being in your mates' pockets and always at the army's beck and call to being able to plan your own day and just do nothing if that's what you want to do! I liked Greece a lot, but I did have trouble looking at the open waters of the sea. This had begun happening to me in the Falklands, in the days after the Sea King had gone down. I felt a heavy weight of grief and sadness when I saw the open water. This in turn made me uncomfortable – these weren't emotions that I wanted to deal with.

I'd have these silly ideas that we'd get the news that the lads had been found alive after swimming to an island and going into survival mode. Of course, as more time passed, that became harder and harder to believe. Eventually I had to accept that those friends and comrades were gone and they weren't coming back. After enough time had passed, I could look at the sea without feeling that sense of terror in my guts. I guess I had come to terms with what had happened.

On 21 July 1982, HMS *Hermes* returned to Portsmouth and thousands of people crammed the dockside to welcome her home, 108 days after she had departed to carry the fight to the enemy. Air superiority – or parity at the very least – is essential for a successful military campaign. Without the aircraft carriers, *Hermes* and the *Invincible*, we would not have been able to retake the islands without losing a savagely high number of ships and men. They had saved a lot of lives.

Flypasts from Army Air Corps Lynx helicopters, Royal Navy Hunter trainer aircraft and Royal Air Force Harriers greeted the ship's crew as they sailed into the harbour, many of them lined up on her decks. It was a scene reminiscent of the Second World War, with the crowds cheering and waving British flags.

Hermes replied to the flybys with a 17-gun salute – a reminder that she had not been away on a jolly, but the business of war. Further evidence of that was the scoreboard on her side, showing a tally of 46 enemy aircraft shot down by her Sea Harriers. Of course, the nature of war is destruction, but 40 years later, it's hard to imagine our troops being allowed to show pride in their kills. These days, it's supposed to be something that you feel sorry about. I can't speak for the Fleet Air Arm pilots, but if I had to guess, I'd say that shooting down the enemy aircraft was one of the best days of their lives for many of them – the pinnacle moment that they had dreamed about and worked for since childhood.

I know that feeling well.

I watched the *Hermes* return to a jubilant Britain on the TV and gave the crew my own salute with a few beers. It was a happy day and I don't think that I've ever seen Britain more united, either before or since. The victory in the Falklands had done more than take back ground, returning it to its rightful people: it had shown the world that Britain not only had the means to go to war, but the will too. No matter the distance or

the dangers, we would stand up for our citizens and our prin-
ciples. It was a shot across the bows to our actual and potential
enemies. I do wonder how much it played into the eventual
peace in Northern Ireland when the terrorists saw what we
were capable of doing when truly let off the leash.

It's a shame that it took a war to bring the country together.
The only other thing that seems to come close is sport, which I
suppose says a lot about man's tribal nature. We seem to need
an 'enemy' and if we can't find one overseas, then we look for
it at home. I don't know if that will ever change. Personally, I
doubt it – not while men are men.

* * *

Back in the summer of 1982, following our return from leave,
the regiment gathered together in the NAAFI for a campaign
debrief. The brigadier was present – no backwards jumper, this
time – as was Colonel Rose. The aim of the debrief was to draw
out lessons learned, but it soon turned into a finger-pointing
session – mostly regarding the aborted or failed missions on
the Argentinian mainland. Things were heating up and the
regimental sergeant major had to step in before things really
escalated. I quite enjoyed the entertainment. All in all, I had
had a good war and I was happy to sit and listen at the debrief
rather than stick my oar in.

Three awards were given out to members of D and G Squadrons. Both squadron commanders received Distinguished

Service Orders and a patrol leader was given the Military Medal. This stood in stark contrast to the Gulf War (January–February 1991), where medals were far more numerous. What a difference a decade makes.

As is the tradition in the regiment, we auctioned off kit belonging to the men who hadn't made it home. The bids were high and all of the money went to the families of the fallen. It was a solemn occasion, but one that was done with a lot of good humour – the best way to honour your mates is to be happy. Tragedy will beset all of us. There's no avoiding it, so laugh while you can.

Jenny and I used to drink most often at The Plough pub in Hereford, the home town of the SAS, and we organised a wake of sorts there to raise a glass to the men who hadn't come home. In particular we remembered Paul Bunker, who used to join us there regularly. I still couldn't quite believe he was gone and I think informal and formal services like this help us to accept and move past tragedy. We will always remember, and it's important that we should, but we can't let life stop when something bad happens. If we did, then we'd never move on at all. Thankfully, the army had taught me that difficult times and challenges were not something to be scared of: things can be tough, so we must be tougher, and life the life we're given.

D and G Squadrons underwent some restructuring. Mountain Troop needed to be rebuilt and Yorkie went across to them from ours. 'Dead man's shoes' needed to be filled and some men saw a chance of moving to Mountain Troop as the possibility to move up the ladder. I don't hold that against them, you have to do what's right for you. Special forces may be a calling, but it's also a job. Certainly, Yorkie's decision bore fruit: after 40 years of service he left the army as a lieutenant colonel.

Our troop commander also moved across to Mountain Troop as he wasn't a big fan of freefalling! Again, no one held that against him. The same cannot be said for the decision making of our high-ranking officers, who decided that any man who was not expected to make the rank of sergeant was to be returned to his original unit instead of being allowed to continue on in the SAS. I thought that was a disgusting decision back then and I still think that way now. Not every man wants rank, and if a trooper is brilliant at his job, what difference if he stays in that role? I felt like it was a case of officers tinkering with something just to try and advance their own career at the expense of other people's. Totally shameful and even worse when you consider that many of those cut were Falklands veterans. They'd done their job and done it well, but apparently that counted for nothing in the eyes of the senior officers.

One of the men we lost to this disgusting policy was Binnsy Evans, who had shot down a Skyhawk with his GPMG – not good enough, apparently! Binnsy was a bloody good soldier who had come to the regiment from 3 RGJ. He had taken part in the Fortuna Glacier OP and the Pebble Island raid. Another victim of this officer's idea was PJ and he was sent back to the unit that he had served with before passing selection and earning his place in the SAS. An unjust decision that still angers me to this day.

The anger that I felt at the end of the war has faded, but does remain. There's still a lot about the war that bothers me, not least the feeling that the Argentinians dragged us into something that they had no intention of seeing out. It just seems like a waste of lives, but I know that there's another side to the coin and that is that I felt incredibly lucky to have had the chance to be a part of the task force. As I met old friends and new throughout the years, I'd come to understand that D Squadron's missions were the envy of many a soldier at home and abroad – after all, how many men get to carry out a textbook raid like we did on Pebble Island? I will always be grateful and proud to have been a part of that. We were given many chances to test ourselves against the enemy and the elements. As a special forces soldier, I'm grateful that I got to be tried by both and not found wanting. I was happy with my conduct in the war. I think my grandfather, my uncles and my dad would all be proud of me for following in their footsteps.

Certainly, I was hungry for more. There was no doubt in my mind that I wanted to continue to serve in 22 SAS. It was my home, my dream, my tribe and my reason for being. Not long after we got back I was offered a six-month posting to Delta Force over in the States. It sounded just what I wanted, but Jenny was none too keen on me leaving again so soon after being away at war and for that reason I turned it down. When you serve, not all the sacrifices you make are for the good of your country. Some you have to make for the sake of your marriage, which has to be a two-way street if it's going to be successful. Jenny and I are still together 40 years later, so we must be doing something right!

Cedric Delves, our officer commanding, went on to a post in the US himself and our new OC started out by giving us a bit of a 'well done, lads' trip to thank the squadron for what we'd done in the Falklands. I imagine also that he wanted us to have some fun, considering we had lost a large number of mates. To that end D Squadron went to Fiji, which is about the most beautiful place on the planet you can imagine. We took some of B Squadron's badged Fijians with us and the plan was that we would do a bit of an army recruiting drive, play rugby, do some adventure training and finish off with an exercise and then a few days' R&R before coming home – sounds good!

Unfortunately, some tiny local rag ran a piece about the trip. The powers that be got wind of it and spat their dummy out, and we were ordered into the Fijian jungle at once. This did not go down well with the blokes, especially as we only had enough ammunition and rations for a short exercise. With that being the case, we spent most of the time sitting around in the jungle doing nothing and during monsoon season too – not fun.

There were a few highlights in the jungle, however. Looking to entertain ourselves, we started to carry out 'hearts and minds' patrols as we would do if we were involved in a counterinsurgency operation. We went to one village which had a picture of Queen Elizabeth II hanging in their long hut. The villagers were as friendly as can be and deeply patriotic and loyal to the Commonwealth. Born of a warrior culture, they wanted to know all the details of the Falklands War. Scobie played the part of Homer and gave them an epic recital about the campaign. The villagers hung on his every word, cheering acts of bravery. It was a flashback to an age when men would leave their lands to fight and those who returned would stand in front of their people and tell them about battles and the heroes that fought them. To a degree, that still existed in the Falklands, but by the time the wars of Afghanistan and Iraq came around, this kind of acceptance of who we are as warriors and warlike peoples seems to have gone away. If you stand up now and say I enjoyed war and I'd like to do it again, most people look at you like you're nuts, but that's the way it's been for thousands of years. People are no different now – we're just told to act differently, that's all.

Meeting the villagers aside, it was a miserable time in the jungle and ended on a tragic note. There was an exercise at the end of the time in the trees, involving a lengthy exfiltration. Unfortunately, the recce on the area had been done in the dry season and it was now monsoons. When we came to

281

what was supposed to be a dry riverbed, we found instead a raging torrent.

Undeterred, the OC ordered us to make rafts with bamboo and we lashed our weapons and kit onto these. Things went well for the first few hundred metres, but then the fast waters took us around a corner and we saw the rapids ahead of us.

Man and raft went through the rocks like they were in a pinball machine. Rafts broke up, weapons were lost and tragically, one of the Fijians drowned in the rapids. Other men pulled themselves up onto boulders and had to be rescued by helicopter winch. It was a fucking disaster to say the least, and a valuable lesson learnt.

Not long after, I was posted to the training wing and I always remember Fiji as an example of what could go wrong.

* * *

As you can imagine, I came across many men on selection who had fought in the Falklands and who had decided they wanted more. I had two lads in my troop who had fought with the Paras at Goose Green and it was interesting to hear stories from the war told from a new angle. They were jealous that we'd done raids and the infantryman in me was jealous that they'd done a battalion attack – c'est la vie!

I was promoted after our return from the Falklands and in 1986 I went back across the water to Northern Ireland, but this time as a team leader. The SAS played a large part in breaking the Provisional Irish Republican Army (PIRA) back in the mid- to late-eighties, but that's a story for another time. What I will say is that I did 15 months straight out there and in that time we chalked up many successes and took terrorists off the streets, both in handcuffs and in body bags.

Our actions on that tour did not go unnoticed. In front of the other troopers and their families in the regimental NAAFI, one of the lads was awarded the British Empire Medal from Prince Charles. I was chuffed for our trooper and then over the moon when I received news that I was to receive my own award. For my accumulated actions in Northern Ireland I would be awarded the Queen's Gallantry Medal and it would be presented by the Queen herself! Well, you can imagine how proud I was to tell my mum and Jenny that I would be taking them to Buckingham Palace to meet Her Majesty.

The papers learned of the award, but didn't print my details when D Squadron told them to stand down. Unlike the other recipients that day, myself and the other troopers could not enter via the public entrance and so we were ushered through the West Wing. It was undergoing renovations, with furniture under cover and the canvasses on the wall gathering dust.

When I met the Queen to be given my award we exchanged a few words about Northern Ireland, but I wasn't particularly blown away by the experience. The first and foremost thought in my mind was that I was proud to have been able to give this experience to my mum. Her happiness and opinion meant a lot more to me than anyone else's. It was the first and last time that I met Her Majesty, but I have always been thoroughly impressed by her. The Queen gives a lot more than she takes and she has done so all her life. People see the palaces and carriages, but how often is she sitting in them with her feet up? Her life is one of service and she has put in a longer stint on behalf of this country than she ever needed to. I think it's a good thing that the armed forces have a figurehead who isn't political. And of course, many of the royal family have put in military service and not just the tick-in-the-box kind. Most recently, Prince Harry was on the front lines in Afghanistan and Prince William flew search-and-rescue Sea Kings. I've travelled a lot in my life and when the royal family have come up in conversation, the general sense from people has been one of intrigue and admiration. You only have to look at the numbers – 1.9 billion people watched the royal wedding of Prince Harry and Meghan Markle. That's almost a third of the world's population and almost double what the World Cup brought in.

I had assumed photos would be taken of my own meeting with royalty and then passed on to us, but I was wrong. Luckily, Del's partner had brought a camera with them and we posed in the deserted West Wing on our way out – that picture of myself and Jenny is still on our living room wall and always will be. I'll be forever indebted to Del and his partner for that!

I was so happy to be able to give my mum that special day. She gripped Jenny's hand like a vice throughout the ceremony, but my wife didn't say anything to spoil the moment, despite grimacing in pain. I had been fortunate enough to have many great days in uniform, but that was certainly one of the best. It was the kind of thing that I'd dreamed of as a boy – a true honour.

I was not done with war, though. In 1991 I deployed again with 22 SAS, this time to the Gulf. Much has been written and spoken about the regiment's role in that war and most of it negative – the books concentrate on the failures, rather than the successful stories. Contrary to the widely held belief, a lot of our missions in the desert went very well. In time, it's something that I would like to talk more about. I am fiercely proud of what we did over there, and of the regiment, and if I can balance the accounts on public opinion, then I will consider that a success.

In total I served 18 years in the Special Air Service and in that time I served in Northern Ireland, the Falklands and the Gulf and trained on several continents. I went all over the world either to teach, or to learn, and sometimes to fight. I served in the desert and in the Antarctic. And while I lost many friends, I made many more.

16

A FINAL WORD

Be kind, for everyone you meet
is fighting a hard battle.

Ian Maclaren, 1897

Taffy was my best friend in the early days of my army career and we kept in touch when I passed selection and moved to Hereford. In fact, Taffy moved there himself when he left the army, becoming a local policeman. He sought me out at the camp and we remained mates.

I'm not sure when things started to go badly for him, or why. Taffy got a divorce, but that wasn't unusual for a soldier or a copper. At one point he asked me for a loan, which I gladly gave him. I didn't ask why he needed it and I have no idea if it was connected to the reasons why he left the police force. A colleague of his told me that Taffy had left the force 'before he was pushed', but that was as much as I heard.

When I heard of his death it was a total shock. It was six months after he passed that I got the news. I was living in the

UAE at the time and the fact that no one had contacted me about the funeral made me very angry. We'd been mates for a long time. Like a lot of brothers in arms, we didn't keep in touch all the time, but when we did, it was as if we'd never been apart. I couldn't believe that he was gone, or that I wouldn't even get the chance to say goodbye to him at his funeral. It was a real kick in the teeth.

Taffy had died of a heart attack in a doctor's office, of all places. He was only 40 years old and he'd been a great athlete in his time, playing rugby for Neath before the army, and a good cricket player after that. It didn't make sense to me then and it doesn't now. Life gives and takes, and very often it takes too soon.

My section commander from my first tour to Northern Ireland, Tony, was also taken before his time. After being shot on a previous tour, Tony had lost his appetite for infantry work and transferred to the Small Arms School Corps (SASC), who train the army's skill-at-arms instructors. Who knows if it was fate or just bad luck, but Tony was killed while testing a new weapons system in Oman. We can all change our paths, but when our time's up, it's up and for some the end comes sooner than others.

I've always been good at shutting things out and I don't dwell on loss. Of course, there are days when I miss people – particularly Taffy and my other close friend Paul Bunker – but I don't let it bring me down. Quite the opposite in fact. I know the blokes wouldn't want me to get miserable and so I don't allow myself to do so. It's as simple as that.

As far as my own mortality goes, I didn't ever particularly worry about dying in the service, but I did wonder about what would come after. As you can imagine, in my kind of work, it was something that would come up in life a lot. Soldiers and military contractors work in an arena of death. Some people are comfortable with it, others not so much. My biggest fear was of being cremated – what if the soul was in the body? Would it suffer? Would I feel pain? In my own life, I've always been proactive. If I wanted something from life, then I'd make it happen. If I wanted answers, then I'd go and look for them. Obviously, getting answers on what comes after this life requires a certain amount of faith and while I had been raised a Christian, I can't say that I felt particularly strongly one way or another. That changed when I spent some time in Texas, not too long ago, and while I won't go into the details, suffice to say I had an experience that made me a believer. My faith was confirmed and I no longer worry about what comes next. Hopefully I've done enough good in my life to earn an admission through the pearly gates.

I believe that D Squadron's OC, Cedric Delves, did a good job of running the squadron at war. Once we were back in the UK he handed over command and went on to a posting at the British Embassy in the United States, acting as a special forces liaison officer. This was almost 20 years before 9/11, but already the special forces communities across the Atlantic were growing closer and Cedric's appointment was one of the steps that led to the close cooperation that continues to this day. Back then I was offered a six-month posting to Delta Force myself, but turned it down to spend more time with Jenny, as described previously. Karl went in my place and had a whale of a time. Over the next few years Air Troop of D Squadron would spend more time working with Delta than any other British unit. Though we serve different countries, I consider them brothers in arms. I was honoured to know many such operators and friends during my time in uniform, but all good things must come to an end.

* * *

I left the Special Air Service in 1996, after 18 years of service, but my time at war was far from over.

The United Arab Emirates had provided the regiment with a Forward Mounting Base during the Gulf War and part of the deal was that we'd give their special forces a five-year training programme to bring them up to a decent level. As things worked out, I managed to see out the last phase of my career as part of that training team and then I extended on in a civilian position. It was a bit different to living in Hereford, but both Jenny and I embraced the change – and the sun!

When the Twin Towers fell in 2001, it was obvious that America would go onto a war footing. Money and conflict go hand in hand and private military companies began popping up across the world like mushrooms. I would work for several of them, with mixed results.

When NATO struck back at Al-Qaeda in Afghanistan, I felt that the missions were thoroughly justified and well executed. A combination of air power, special forces units and local forces were being used to smash Al-Qaeda and most of the battles were taking place in the mountains, away from civilian settlements where a badly judged air strike could turn the tide of support against us.

I didn't feel the same way about the invasion of Iraq in 2003. I didn't believe the claims that President Saddam Hussein could strike Britain, or that he had any intention of doing so. Nor did I believe that he would work with Al-Qaeda founder Osama bin Laden, as Saddam's rule rested on a secular power where people pledged allegiance to the state, rather than to religion. It seemed pretty obvious that America's leaders wanted the war and no one was willing to tell them no.

For a private contractor like me, Iraq was a big pay day. In the early days the money was good, but it soon became clear that the risks would be high. There had been a moment of peace following the toppling of the regime, but anyone with an ounce of knowledge about the region could see that this was the calm before the storm. Jihadi fighters began flooding in from across the world to take a crack at the forces who had invaded a Muslim country. Iran began to back Shia militias. Saudi Arabia and the UAE backed Sunni militias. With Saddam's monopoly on power up for grabs, those militias, tribes, sects and foreign powers began jostling for supremacy. It was a recipe for disaster and the one hope to stop it boiling over was the Iraqi army.

Iraq still had a huge number of young men under arms and in units. If they could be used to keep order – as they had under Saddam, but now with a new mandate – then the country might have been saved the civil war that still racks it to the time of writing, 18 years later. When the Americans ordered that the Iraqi army be dismantled, they doomed the country to endless suffering and I can't help but wonder if they did so deliberately – a lot of American companies and politicians have done very nicely out of the chaos.

I was in Iraq in 2003 and I saw the writing on the wall. As I say, it wasn't difficult to see, which is what leads me to think that the chaos was caused deliberately. At the time I was working in Baghdad for Motorola, advising on security for our Arab technicians. A lot of them were staying at the Lebanon Hotel, but I saw this as a very soft target and asked for them to be moved into housing in the Mansoor district of the city. Thankfully, the company took notice as a 500lb car bomb was detonated outside of the Lebanon, killing 23, including the UN's top envoy to Iraq – the UN Commissioner for Human Rights – Sergio Vieira de Mello of Brazil.

After six months I left the Motorola gig to go and work on CPATT, which was US Army General Petraeus's plan to train up the new Iraqi security forces. The only Brit on the team, I was working with Americans to train up the emergency response unit. Our recruits were brave and believed in the mission. They had to or they wouldn't be there, as it was an incredibly dangerous job. Many Iraqis died on the day that they went to sign up, killed by car bombs as they lined up at the recruiting stations, or ambushed as they were taken on buses to training. After almost two decades of war, I doubt many of the men we trained are alive today.

Obviously, as a soldier, I am not opposed to war, but I do feel that the armed forces have been used and abused in recent decades and that the military covenant has not been honoured.

The Good Friday Agreement, as the peace deal in Northern Ireland was known, was a real kick in the teeth. The SAS had done a huge part in breaking PIRA's back in the eighties, but there was almost a decade of waffling by politicians before they finally sealed the deal on 10 April 1998. It wasn't a nice feeling to see terrorists being pardoned and allowed to walk out from jail and at first I could at least tell myself that it was the price to pay for peace. It was a lot harder to keep my cool when the witch-hunts started to go after British soldiers, which is nothing less than disgusting. I'm not saying that soldiers don't ever make mistakes, but I can't stomach the fact that it's OK to pardon terrorists and not grant that same clemency to the soldiers who went to war on Britain's behalf.

I spent a spell living in Texas between 2004 and 2010 and America sets a good standard for looking after its veterans. I'm sure they also have room for improvement in their Veterans Administration, but little things that they offer, like VA loans, are a great idea. The best thing that America does for its veterans is to offer the GI Bill, which goes towards – and sometimes covers – a veteran's university education and their housing while they study. I think this is a great idea as a lot of soldiers join the military without much in the way of academic qualifications. This is usually down to a lack of opportunity rather than intelligence. Giving a soldier a chance to gain those qualifications after service benefits the veteran and society because the veteran brings their insights into the business world. As it is, a large proportion of veterans go into the security world, or some form of manual work. It would be great to see something like the GI Bill introduced in Britain, but I don't think it's something that the Ministry of Defence will ever supply.

Mental health is obviously talked about a lot now, including around veterans, but it just wasn't discussed at the time when I served. I'm sure some people did suffer, but if they did then they did so quietly and out of sight. Speaking for myself, I was saddened to lose comrades but I didn't suffer from flash-backs and nightmares. Perhaps if the Sea King had gone down at the end of the war, when the job was done, it would have been harder to stomach, but as it was we got an opportunity to throw ourselves into action not long after that loss and I think that's very important. It's the old wisdom about getting back in the saddle once a horse has thrown you off. We weren't given time to dwell and we were given an opportunity to avenge our fallen comrades – that's all a soldier can ask for.

I feel bad for any veteran living on the street, or struggling with their mental health, but I'd feel just the same way if they were a civilian. As a society, there's a lot of room across the board to improve how we take care of each other and ourselves. I think the UK government could do better, but at the same time I'm not angry at them. If we're honest, we could all do better, couldn't we? The SAS is made up of individuals who have proved that they can work well on their own, but it's only when we come together as a unit that we can pull off operations like the Pebble Island raid, or the 1980 Iranian Embassy hostage rescue. We need to adopt that same mentality as a society: everyone trying to reach their own personal potential, but coming together to do even bigger and better things. No man is an island, no matter how much we might like to think that way. With such thoughts in mind, I decided that I would attend the 2021 Remembrance Parade in London, something that I had never done before.

Remembrance Day is one of – if not *the* – most important date in the British calendar. Everything that we have in the United Kingdom is built on a foundation of freedom and that foundation was bought and paid for with the lives of thousands upon thousands of people. It is incredibly important that we remember what they gave up, not just so that we can be grateful for their sacrifice, but so that we do not repeat the mistakes of the past. What rational civilisation would ever want to go through another Battle of the Somme? If we don't remember lessons then we are doomed to repeat them.

Remembrance Day is of course a time when I remember my own fallen comrades, but I take solace in knowing that they died doing what they loved. When I think about my father's generation, it's a bit different: many of those men answered the call of war, but would have been quite content never to see any conflict. The fact that they did not seek it out makes them all the braver in my eyes. Imagine growing up wanting to be a teacher, but instead you feel like you have no choice in picking up a rifle and going ashore in Normandy, or fighting through Burma. A lot of people ask me if warriors are born, or made, and when I think of Britain's service personnel in the two world wars, I think the answer makes itself very obvious: both.

I joined 10,000 other veterans for the Remembrance Parade in London. There were a lot of grey hairs, but plenty of smiles! Stick a veteran in a parade and he is transported back in time to the person he was as a soldier. The memories come flooding back. It's easy to forget just who you were, and what you did, but as you hear the military bands play and listen to the blokes' banter, you soon realise that this was where you were always meant to be.

It sounds idyllic, but that's the truth. Maybe it's not so much that we are born for war, but born to be in the company of soldiers. I'm sure, if you gave a lot of us a choice, we would spare the death and destruction so long as we could still have the friendships and bonds that we had developed in uniform.

On my ticket for the day was a column number and I found someone holding up a sign for the Royal Green Jackets. I looked around the faces and was disappointed that I didn't recognise anyone, which wasn't a shock given that I had served 50 years ago, but still a bit of a shame. I also realised that I had forgotten to bring my medals, but that wasn't a bad thing: given that we were told that we couldn't wear the sand-coloured beret of the SAS, my medals would have stuck out a mile among the solo Northern Ireland medal of most of the veterans – they might have thought I was some sort of Walter Mitty!

In all honesty, it did annoy me that we were told not to wear special forces berets. I'd worked bloody hard to earn mine, as has every other SF soldier. There's no way they would ever tell the airborne not to wear maroon lids, or Commandos their green berets, so why not allow it for the SAS? I have my own suspicions but I'll keep those to myself, ha! And it didn't put any kind of a dampener on the day. I suppose we are always boy soldiers at heart, no matter our age, and I felt the old thrill as I heard the band strike up and we were given the order to march.

It is always an incredible feeling to be part of something bigger than yourself. After service it is easy to go through life thinking about the world through a very small prism. When we retook the South Atlantic islands I knew I was a part of history and a part of a fraternity that would bond myself and strangers for life. While the Remembrance Parade was not to that same level of intensity, it pressed the same buttons and it was hard work to keep a smile off my face and maintain a slight scowl as befits a marching infantry soldier!

The Green Jackets were the second-to-last regiment to pass the reviewing stand, where Prince William was taking the salute. Much to my delight we were ordered to break into the light infantry's drill, paced at 140 steps a minute. Well, I did wonder if people's tickers could take it and I must admit that it got the blood pumping, but I didn't see anyone fall down or trip over everyone, so I think the old boys did alright!

The ceremony took place at its annual location at the Cenotaph on Whitehall, London, and it was a suitably solemn occasion. The 'Last Post' was played and I thought about the comrades that I had lost in war, but also strangers. Men and women that I will never meet, but to whom I owe a debt of gratitude and hold in the highest regard.

It was an honour to take part in the service. It was something I had always wanted to do and recent events have shown that we can't take things for granted. Who knows what the future holds, but however things shake out, remembrance must be something that we as a nation always hold dear.

After the service I met up with a mate of mine from my days on the circuit. There was a great buzz around the place as thousands of veterans swapped stories and banter. I would have loved to have stayed and got on the pints, but I had to leave to be elsewhere that afternoon. Nonetheless, it was a day that will stay with me forever.

We will remember them.

* * *

Today it is common for people to think of those who served in the SAS as heroes, but the only heroes in the regiment are the dead. The rest of us are just ordinary men who were asked to do extraordinary things in extraordinary times. Nothing more and nothing less.

When asked if the Falklands War was justified, I have no hesitation in saying yes. Thousands of British citizens were being held hostage on the islands. We went there to liberate them and to continue to give them a path of self-determination – one where they continually and overwhelmingly vote to remain a territory of the United Kingdom. If that changes, so be it, but it is the islanders' right to choose who governs them and I am proud to have done my part in restoring that.

As with every war, there are certain conspiracies that surface. One of which is that HMS *Invincible* was struck by a bomb from an A4 Skyhawk. For some reason, Argentinians believe that we denied this strike. Their reasoning? Because the pilot said so and because the *Invincible* didn't return to the UK until September of 1982

Now I've never flown a jet at high speed, low altitude and into the face of enemy anti-aircraft fire, but I think I can make a guess that those are pretty confusing conditions. We don't have the massive carriers that America does and I think it would be quite possible to mistake another ship for the *Invincible*. Besides, why would Britain – and the entire crew of the ship – pretend that the carrier hadn't been damaged? There's no claim by Argentina that it was sunk. We lost several ships, so it's not like the British public needed to be shielded from the news that our navy was under threat. We knew that all too well. Total bollocks, ha ha!

The other, more grizzly conspiracy theory is that atrocities took place by both sides. Obviously, I was not present all over the islands and at every engagement, but I did spend a long time in the military and later working as a private military contractor. I have been around Falkland veterans all my life and I have never come across anyone with first-hand knowledge of atrocities by either side. I'm sure there were some people killed in the fighting who didn't have a weapon in their hands, but that is the chaos of hand-to-hand fighting at night-time, on a mountain – not war crimes. War is a chaotic, ugly business. As I've said before, the only way to avoid such deaths is to avoid war.

The MOD took the claims seriously enough to put a historical war crimes team on the case in the early nineties and they found nothing. Personally, I find these teams quite an awful idea. Imagine having your actions in bloody, brutal combat picked over decades later by someone who has all the time in the world to think, when you didn't even have a split second to make your decision. It is political meddling by people who will send young people to fight and die, but who have never stood in the firing line themselves.

Yes, I am bitter about certain things, but please don't think that these grievances overshadow the good, because they do not. Not by a long shot. I take great pride in being a Falklands veteran and it is an honour to have a common bond with the infantry who performed so remarkably on the islands. There was never a backward step and they carried all in front of them despite the conditions and the enemy's superior positions on the high ground. I believe that the British soldier was the best-trained infantryman in the world in 1982 and even though we are generations apart, I think Afghanistan and Iraq have proved that our nation is not short of war-fighters who could do it all again if asked. In every generation there are warriors made for the life and the British Army has the training to mould these people into the best soldiers in the world.

I don't miss being in the army, but I do miss working with small, professional teams of warriors. The itch is always there to go back. Once I put down my pen on this book, I will be travelling to Libya for another bite of the apple. I was destined to travel and born for war. Of course, I was not the only one and as I close this book I wish to thank my fellow Falkland veterans for their courage and professionalism.

We did alright, didn't we?

Onwards and upwards!

ACKNOWLEDGEMENTS

There are several acknowledgements that I must make in this book but I will keep it brief.

Firstly to Gez Jones who helped me pen this book. Gez is an accomplished writer and his experience as a Military Veteran shone through and made an ordinary story great. I thank him for it. I look forward to future collaborations together.

To 'All Arms Services' that made Operation Corporate a success. Your professionalism and spirit won the day and I salute you all.

To the man who put me in touch with my editor at Welbeck Publishing. Once again thank you for the help you gave me, as you did Jenny. Not forgotten.

To the Dead. You are the Heroes, not us. Let us not forget them and their sacrifice on the sea and the wind-swept hillsides of the Falkland Islands far from home. I did not believe then their sacrifice was in vain and I do not now.

Lastly to my long-suffering wife Jenny. You waited so long then, as you still do at times now. Your love remains with me whereever I go and I thank God daily for meeting you long ago in Hereford when things were not great. Thanks for 'Fluencing Away' the bad times. Thankfully there has not been many. 'Always Yours'.